NOBODY'S DAUGHTER

Dr. Stacey Nickleberry

This book is a work of non-fiction. However, some names have been changed to protect identities of certain individuals. Any similarities to events of others' lives are not the intentions of the author and are purely coincidental.

All included Bible scriptures are from the King James Version of the Bible, unless otherwise noted.

Published by CLF PUBLISHING, LLC. 3281 E. Guasti Road, Seventh Floor, Ontario, CA 91761. (760) 669-8149.

Copyright © 2014 by Stacey Nickleberry. All rights reserved. No portion of this book may be reproduced, stored in a retrieval system, or transmitted by any form or any means electronically, photocopied, recorded, or any other except for brief quotations in printed reviews, without the prior permission of the publisher.

Cover Design by Senir Design. Contact information- info@senirdesign.com.

ISBN #978-0-9960815-2-8

Printed in the United States of America.

Dedications

I dedicate this book to my mother Betty Ann Hunter Gillespie.

Most importantly, I dedicate this book to all females who experienced a fatherless home, resulting in a destructive path, which contributed to emptiness in their hearts and souls.

Acknowledgements

I acknowledge the following individuals:

My late great-grandmother Nana, who taught me to pray and introduced me to Jesus Christ, the Savior and Lord of my life. My grandmother Ora Lee, who taught my mother and me how to be strong women. My mother Betty Ann, who taught me to be strong in the Lord, to never give up regardless of the circumstances or how hopeless a situation may appear, and to never depend on anyone made of flesh and blood. Enormous thanks to my pastors and teachers for teaching the word of God without compromising the truth. My children, LaVon, Jacque, Tyese, Turron, Melva, and Melvin Jr. who love me unconditionally. To my brother and sisters, know that I have forgiven you and will continually pray for your salvation. To my grandchildren, JaNiece, Jasmine, Keyerrah Timothy, and Adaorah; Grandma loves you. To my great-grandson, Frank Noble V and my great-granddaughter, My'ale. I love you and pray for you daily. A special thanks to my cousins: Michael Gregory and Sundeana Gregory Johnson, special supporters: Henry Johnson, Jr., Willie Saulberry, Patricia Linguard Wilkerson, and Robert (Poochie) Johnson, and finally to all those who read my book and believe: Psalms 91:1- **He who dwells in the Secret place of the Most High shall remain stable and fixed under the shadow of the Almighty whose power no foe can withstand (**Amplified Bible).

I also want to acknowledge my biological family. It is understandable because we were never introduced you don't know me personally. Regardless of whatever you were told, hopefully after you have read my book, you will come to your own conclusion. I make no apologies to any family members because you have your own memories, and they are your reality. I'm asking for you to just accept mine because it is equally as valid.

Preface

We all enter this world innocent in the natural but condemned in the spiritual realm. We often wonder if this is all life has to offer or could there be something more. We wonder why our lives, our attitudes, emotions, position in life, wealth or lack thereof is the way it is. We may have been successful in our adult lives contributing these assets to our forefathers, good parenting, or our self-determination. We may still wonder why there is still a void in ourhearts or our inner being. Maybe even with all our prestige, wealth, and position, we still feel something is missing.

Please bear with me, while I tell my story about my life, my trials, my tribulations, my ups and downs, those that I loved, and those I didn't know how to love. Maybe at the end of my story, you may reach the same conclusion, which took me years to understand, comprehend, and decide that I did the BEST I could with the hand I was dealt.

I was raised to believe God had a purpose and there is always a plan. Some people will find the truth and accomplish their purpose sooner than others. Some of us need a helping hand, a mentor, a spiritual mentor, and our Heavenly Father leading and guiding our steps, ever so gently. When you find your purpose, I am certain the void in your heart will transform and your new life will begin. Get comfortable while you begin to read my journey and the purpose for this book: to understand how I have come to have peace with myself and the people whom I love and who love me, as I am. I understand there is no greater love than the love of our Heavenly Father. Realizing this, I am eternally grateful.

Table of Contents

Introduction	9
Chapter 1 *Before I was Born*	13
Chapter 2 *YHWH is Your Guardian*	15
Chapter 3 *Everyone has Troubles*	19
Chapter 4 *Understanding Your Ancestors and Their Life*	21
Chapter 5 *Grandmother Lee and My Trip to California*	29
Chapter 6 *Walking in a Fog...Not Knowing the Reasons*	33
Chapter 7 *Wives' Tales from New Orleans*	37
Chapter 8 *Growing Up in the Fifties in Gary, Indiana*	41
Chapter 9 *A Change in My Environment*	47
Chapter 10 *My First Trip to New Orleans*	49
Chapter 11 *Not Only My Heritage, but also My Cultural Experiences*	57
Chapter 12 *Gaining Spiritual Insight in Church*	59
Chapter 13 *Life with the Only Dad I Knew*	61
Chapter 14 *Why Don't I Have My Own Father?*	67

Chapter 15 *My Elementary and Junior High Era*	69
Chapter 16 *Summertime*	71
Chapter 17 *And Suddenly No Father*	77
Chapter 18 *High School Days*	79
Chapter 19 *Being Nobody's Daughter has a Negative Effect*	85
Chapter 20 *Teenage Social Life*	87
Chapter 21 *Pre-College Days: Partying Until I Dropped*	93
Chapter 22 *Our First African American Mayor*	97
Chapter 23 *College Days: Indiana University*	101
Chapter 24 *Married too Young*	107
Chapter 25 *Not Having Nana was Too Much for Me to Bear*	111
Chapter 26 *Closing Thoughts*	129
About the Author	131
References	132

Introduction

"I will always love you no matter what," "You can always talk to me," "You're beautiful," "You're smart," and "I love you more than anything" are words I never heard while growing up from my biological father. I cannot say I was ever physically abused by my biological father, but I was extremely mentally damaged. On the other hand, you may have been raised in an abusive home environment where you heard, "You're not good for anything," "You're ugly," "You're stupid," or "Nobody wants you." Or, someone may have said he/she wished you were dead. You may have been molested by a family member or a stranger. You may have experienced abandonment, neglect, been battered, or lied to because of hidden agendas. Family lies and curses may have come from those who claimed to love you but cared more about themselves ormore about what others might think.

I want this book to minister to all women whose fathers were missing in action and not a part of their upbringing. I call these women "bruised souls." After many years, I finally realized there is someone far greater than any human on this earth that can mend a broken-heart, fill the hole in a soul, and restore the years that the locust has eaten. (Locust is the most destructive insect; it eats everything in its path, leaving nothing.) That one someone is Our Lord and Savior and His Son, the Son of the living God.

I have often wondered why I kept going around the same mountain as I did for the majority of my life. My mountains were trying to find love in all the wrong places and trying to make each man I met my daddy. That was an impossible mission and was difficult because I never knew what a real daddy does, and what I was looking for only existed in my mind.

Even if you had a father, he was not perfect. How do you create a father if you have no idea how one is supposed to behave? Therefore, I went looking for a man I thought would be like a father, or who possessed qualities and behaviors I associated with a father. What a frustrating expedition.

I was building a Frankenstein. How crazy!

Now, as an adult, I have wondered from where all my anger originated. I had grown bitter at the world due to the absence of my birth father in my life. I always felt something was missing. I later realized how important it is in a young girl's life to have a relationship with her father while growing up. I often wondered how my life would have been different with my biological father in my life. Anger made me blame everything wrong in my life on my father; who else was I to blame? Over and over, my father was the blame for everything, until the point, I never wanted a father in my life. So I rehearsed this thought over and over with every essence of my being. Maybe, I did that so much just to see if my Heavenly Father would reject me also.

Deuteronomy 1:6 says, *"The Lord our God said to us in Horeb, You have dwelt long enough on this mountain."*

You may be thinking, *This book has nothing to do with me.* Or, you may be saying, "I am not angry." Well, let me ask you a couple

of questions, and if you can answer yes to any of these, please continue reading this book.
- Have you been married more than twice?
- Are you satisfied with your current position in life?
- Is there emptiness in your heart and nothing seems to fill the void?

If you answered yes to any of those three questions, you need to continue reading.

Most people believe that if you do not look or feel angry, then you do not have an anger problem or issues. Anger is not something you can see. It is feelings and behaviors contributed to emotions you have not addressed or may not understand.

Symptoms of Anger

1. Explosive outbursts leading to physical attacks or destruction of property.
2. Exaggerate hostility to unimportant irritants.
3. Rapid and harsh statements of judgment made to or about others.
4. Use of body language, such as tense muscles, clenched fist or jaw, glaring or refusal to make eye contact.
5. Use of passive-aggressive behaviors.
6. Social withdrawal due to anger.
7. Refusing to complete assignments in a timely manner.
8. Refusing to follow instructions or rules.
9. Complaining about authority figures behind their backs.
10. Refusing to participate in activities when the above behaviors are anticipated.
11. Authority is challenged or disrespected.
12. Abusive language is utilized.

(swayamsat.org/blog.item.20/signs-symptoms-of-anger.html)

A few years ago, I would have argued with anyone if it were suggested that I had an anger issue or even a problem. I realized I had an anger problem when I sought God and He slowly showed me incidents in my life. With His holy guidance, I began weeding out my hurting soul. Believe me, it was not an easy task, and God is not finished with me yet. I fought God on many occasions. Yes, I was fighting with my Heavenly Father and sometimes tried to correct Him, as though He had me mixed up with someone else. I struggled to get to understand the ***"ROOT"*** of the issues at hand. (I want to say here, God doesn't remember your past nor does He beat you over your head. However, He knew what I needed at certain periods of time to get me aligned to His plans for my life.) As I said, this was a slow process. It has taken my entire life to get over the hurt and abuse I suffered. However, God's mercy, grace, and His cleansing blood washed me clean. Thanks to God!

You can experience liberation and fulfillment of the love of God, hopefully through reading my life experiences and how I overcame the feelings of hurt, abuse, and anger. Genesis 2:7 says, **"And the Lord God formed man of the dust of the ground, and breathed into his nostrils the breath of life; and man became a living soul."**

Chapter 1
Before I was Born

My mom and dad both attended Roosevelt High School in Gary, Indiana. In fact, in the 1940's, that was the only school they could attend. Soon after my biological dad graduated from high school, he joined the army, and my mother went off to attend Lincoln University, in Lincoln, Missouri. I do not know how or when my mother became pregnant, but that is another story. My mom quit college because she was pregnant and moved to New Orleans with her mother's sister, my great aunt Clara, until I was born. Too bad there was not a television program back in the day called Maury because I can hear my biological father's mother saying, "He is not the baby's father!" Whatever! I never liked that two-faced woman, and I felt her feelings concerning me were mutual.

My mother before I was born

Dr. Stacey Nickleberry

The Beginning

Hurricane STACEY arrived in New Orleans, Louisiana at 5:27pm, on October 10, 19?? I do not remember if anyone was prepared for my arrival or had any idea of the destruction and havoc I would create later in life. Many just thought another Negro baby girl was born to an ordinary Negro mother named Ann. I really do not think my Negro father was there, as he never showed up to anything important in my life, unless there was something in it for him.

My earliest memory of my destructive behavior and stubbornness is of one very hot summer day. I believe I was two years old. I was sitting on Nana's (my great-grandmother) porch steps. The temperature was over 90 degrees, in Gary, Indiana. I remember my mother calling me and saying, "Stacey, come inside. It's too hot outside, and you're going to get black." At the time, I had no idea what black was. It sounded as if it was something bad. In my own little stubbornness, I thought, *Whatever or whoever black is, I want to stay outside until black comes.* I quickly responded to my mother's call, "I ain't hot and don't want to come inside. I want to wait for Black." As you may guess, I heard that story every holiday our family members gathered. Nana would laugh so hard about that story until tears would fill her eyes.

Proverbs 6:22- **"When you go, they {the words of your parents' God} shall lead you; when you sleep, they shall keep you; and when you waken, they shall talk with you"** (Amplified).

(Note: I am using the word Negro because this is what Blacks/African Americans were referred to in 1940-1960's.)

Chapter 2
YHWH is Your Guardian

Deuteronomy 1:30- *"The LORD your God, who goes before you, He will fight for you, according to all He did for you in Egypt before your eyes."*

I remember my great-grandmother Nana. Her name was Rebecca Tolbert, but I called her 'My Nana' because I wanted everyone to know she belonged exclusively to me. Her husband worked in the Gary US Steel Mill, and he had a heart attack before I was born. I heard nothing but good things about him, such as how he worked hard and was a good provider. He had moved Nana and their daughter Grandmother Lee from Buffalo, New York to Minnesota and finally to Gary, Indiana. A white man in Minnesota told my great-grandfather about Gary, while he was shopping for shoes for Grandma Lee. Back then, Negroes could not try on shoes. They just had to measure their feet and hope they bought the right size. Also, there were no exchanges for Negroes back then. I suppose white people thought they would get a "disease" if they wore anything after a Negro person. That white fellow told Great-Grandpa about the jobs that were available for Negro folk in Indiana. Gary was located near Lake Michigan and East Chicago. I can imagine, my great-grandpa, like the Beverly Hillbillies, going home that evening and announcing, "We are moving to Indiana."

Once in Indiana, my great-grandparents settled in Gary, into a boarding house on 24th and Adams. It was a mixed neighborhood of Negroes and Eastern Europeans. It was during the Great Depression or soon after. A white fellow sold the boarding house to my great-grandparents; it was God's plan. I loved that house while growing up; there were so many bedrooms to play in. The house also had a basement, but I never liked to play there.

A Strong Foundation

It is what you cannot see that hurts you. What little girl growing up understands a family if all she sees is Grandma? There is no one coming home after work saying to her, "Daddy is home."

I loved me some Nana. She would tell me things that I am just getting the revelation of today. Nana taught me how to read from the Holy Bible and told me about Jesus Christ at a very early age. We would listen to Reverend Ike, Dr. Vernon McGee, and Oral Roberts on the radio. I believed my great-grandmother loved Reverend Ike the most, because she would get the handkerchief out that he had mailed to her every time he came across the radio airwaves. Revered Ike always talked about healing and wealth. At the time, I did not know why healing and wealth were important.

Nana did not work outside the home. Occasionally, she would cook for her Baptist church functions. My great-grandparents rented bedrooms out to single Negro men who worked in Gary's Steel Mill. During that time, men from the south where moving up North for better opportunities, either working in the Gary Steel Mills or factories along the Great Lakes. Nana would wash their clothes and cook for them, in return for them paying her money for room and board.

As I think about that old boarding house, I remember Nana's furnace used coal; later, she had it converted to gas. The coal truck would pull up to the house (before the furnace was converted) and shovel coal into the shoot that led to the basement. Then, Nana would go to the basement and shovel the coal into the furnace. One day, the coal man told Nana he thought someone was living on the side of her house. To my surprise, the next day, Nana got up early the next morning and caught a man sleeping on the side of the house. He had made himself a bed out of cardboard. He told Nana he did not have any money and his payday would be next week from the Steel Mill. He also told her that one of the men in the boarding house had told him about Nana's Boarding House. Nana let him stay in one of the rooms after he took a bath, until he received his first paycheck. In the meantime, Nana had him cut the grass and do some chores around the house for his room and food.

I asked Nana why a person would want to live outside. She said, "During the Great Depression, many people lost their jobs and their savings, because they had trusted the banks. Many people also lost their homes. It was harder on white people than Negroes, because Negroes were already living in a 'Depression' before the news got to them." We just did not have a word for hard times, but we always seemed to be in hard times anyway.

Amongst the great wealth of information Nana shared with me, she told me about "Share Croppers," in the South; they were dirt poor. Some Negroes were brought into a system that was not designed to assist Negroes out of poverty but to keep them confined and in the South. (It was an extension of slavery). During the Gilded Age, many African Americans and whites lacked the money to buy farmland and farm supplies. They became tenant farmers and sharecroppers. Tenant farmers usually paid the landowner rent for farmland and a house. They owned the crops they planted and made their own decisions about them. After harvesting the crop, the tenant sold it and received income from it. From that income, he paid the landowner the amount of rent owed. Over the years, low crop yields and unstable crop prices forced more farmers into tenancy. The crop-lien system kept many in an endless cycle of debt and poverty. Between 1880 and 1900, the number of tenants increased from 53,000 to 93,000. By 1890, one in three white farmers and three of four black farmers were either tenants or sharecroppers (http://history1800s.about.com/od/1800's glossary/g/Sharecropping-def.htm).

They would work the farms raising cotton, tobacco, sugarcane or peanuts for a percentage of the money from the harvest only to get cheated out of the profit after their so-called expenses were deducted. That system made many Negroes dependent upon a system that could not possibly work, a system not much better than slavery. It is similar to the credit card system we have today. In addition, some of us are still living in the Babylon System of Economy instead of God's economy, where we depend upon God's economic plan for our lives. (Babylon means man-made system instead of allowing God to provide for our needs.)

Chapter 3
Everyone has Troubles

Nana, as best as I can remember, always lent a helping hand. She stood on the Bible verse Psalm 37:25- **"I have been young, and now am old; yet I have not seen the righteous forsaken, nor his descendants begging bread."**

Nana was a faithful member of First Baptist Church and sang in the choir. Nana cooked for funerals and other church functions. When somebody in the church died, Nana would fry chicken and cook collard greens and cornbread for the family. Nana did not like funerals. She said she could always tell when someone went to heaven or hell. Nana said, "If the person went to heaven, I will see a white glow around the coffin, and if the person went to hell, there will be darkness around the coffin." Nana could see things other folks could not. (I think Nana just made up some of her stories).

Nana also told me about hobo living. Some men would hop trains going from place to place trying to find work. These men were called "hobos." Today, we call these people "homeless."

Hobos are popularly thought of as wearing tattered rags, with a sooty face and carrying a bundle fashioned from a stick and a bandana with all their earthly goods. This image is partly due to comedians, such as Red Skelton and Charlie Chaplin who cultivated this image with characters, such as 'Freddie the Freeloader' and 'The Little Tramp'. In fact, hobos were and are as diverse in appearance as any other slice of the human race. Hobos live on a combination of hand-outs, theft and when possible, work.

Within the hobo community, there is some controversy as to whether or not a true hobo works. Some hobo authorities believe a non-worker is never truly a hobo, but rather is a tramp, or bum. Tramps or bums essentially live outside of the law and would be just as likely to rob someone as to ask for food. Unfortunately, hobo-on-hobo crimes occur very frequently, ranging from theft to rape and murder. Most hobos seem to have a common bond though and work together for their mutual survival. In the early 1900s, the growing fraternity of hobos developed an intricate system of graffiti (or 'hobo signs') to give travelling tips to other hobos. Four prongs inside a rectangle on a fence indicate that an ill-tempered dog inhabits that yard. A top hat and triangle may indicate that a family is wealthy. An X inside of a circle would mean that the place is ripe for a handout. Of course, just as with any language, hobo signs vary slightly from place to place (Hobo History, Jack London).

In addition to learning an abundance of history from Nana, I also learned a bit from Grandma Lee. I called Nana's daughter Grandma Lee, for she was my grandmother. She worked on the railroad trains in Chicago. She would tell me how the white people would call all the Negro men "George," even though that was not their name. I never asked what they called the Negro women, who cleaned and mopped the trains like Grandma Lee.

Chapter 4
Understanding Your Ancestors and Their Life

Genesis 8:22- *"While the earth remaineth, seedtime and harvest, and cold and heat, and summer and winter, and day and night shall not cease."*

My grandma Ora Lee was born around 1897, and she had seen all the misery one needed to see. She wanted to be a Harlem Show Girl, but Nana, a Christian woman, would not permit it. Grandma Lee worked several jobs before she began cleaning trains as a railroad worker. In this book, I have included information concerning the conditions in which she was brought up and the life she experienced in America.

The full story of the Pullman Porter is worthy of many exhibits. To say the least, Pullman porters had a hard, demanding, and often dangerous job dealing with a wide variety of problems. Porters were occasional targets of physical abuse, often suffered from verbal and mental abuse, and had to deal with "gun-toting lunatics," robbers, and accidents on top of the very difficult and never-ending tasks of their day-today job.

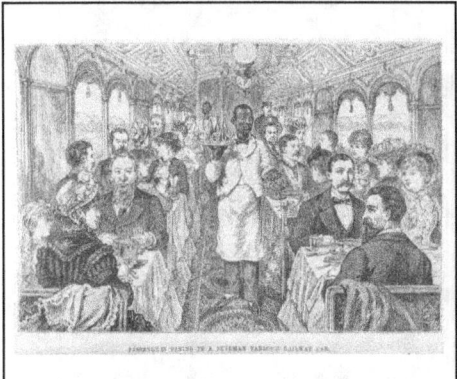

In the early 20th century, porters were dependent on tips for much of their income; that, in turn, made them dependent on the whims of white passengers. Porters spent roughly ten percent of their time in unpaid set-up and clean-up duties, and they had to pay for their food, lodging, and uniforms. Additionally, money was deducted from their pay whenever their passengers stole a towel or a water pitcher. Porters could ride at half fare on their days off - but not on Pullman coaches. Advancements did not exist; therefore, they were unable to obtain promotions to better paying jobs, such as the position of conductor, a job reserved for whites, even though they frequently performed many of the conductor's duties.

Casual Racism ~~Is that such a thing?

White America viewed people of color as inferior, who were ridiculed and scorned. Entertainment media would think nothing of portraying black Americans as cartoon-like savages in offensive popular portrayals. An example of this was seen in popular music of the time:

Outright Prejudice

Casual racism easily spilled over into ugly and random violence. "Jim Crow" segregation laws were designed to keep the races separated during Pullman car travel. The Chicago Defender (An African American owned newspaper) reported stories of brutal and humiliating treatment of Negroes, south of the Mason/Dixon line, in Arkansas and in Oklahoma.

"Porters Are Clubbed and Put Off Train"
The Chicago Defender
October 20, 1917

"Eject Couple From Pullman"
The Cleveland Advocate
October 14, 1916

"Chicago Woman and Children Mistreated"
The Chicago Defender
July 29, 1917

"Forced to Ride In Day Coach"
The Chicago Defender March

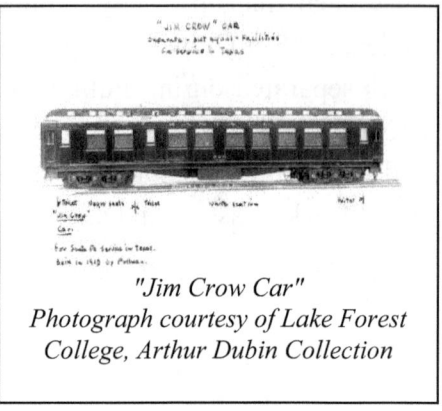

"Jim Crow Car"
Photograph courtesy of Lake Forest College, Arthur Dubin Collection

"Quit Begging for Social Equality"
The Chicago Defender
September 2, 1911

Who Was Jim Crow?

The term "Jim Crow" is used when describing the onerous segregation laws that arose after Reconstruction ended in 1877 and continued until the mid-1960's. The term "Jim Crow" actually began as a song, written by Thomas 'Daddy' Rice in 1828. Rice, a struggling New York actor, became rich and famous overnight by portraying the character Jim Crow, a highly stereotyped, cruelly exaggerated African-American character. Rice was credited with originating the practice of minstrel shows, appearing with a face blackened with cork on stages across America. By 1838, the term was known as a racial epithet for African Americans. Rice squandered his fortune and died in poverty in New York City in September 1860.

Cover to early edition of <u>Jump Jim Crow</u> sheet music
Thomas D. Rice is pictured in his blackface role; he was performing at the Bowery Theatre (also known as the "American Theatre") at the time.

Fighting Back

At some point, people simply had had enough-- of violence, inferior service, and humiliation. African-American porters and passengers alike began to chip away at the Jim Crow regulations;

however, it was not until the Civil Rights Act of 1964 that the "separate but equal" laws, at least as they pertained to interstate travel on rail service and later buses, began to be repealed.

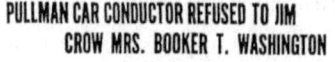

"Pullman Car Conductor Refuses to Jim Crow Mrs. Booker T. Washington"
The Chicago Defender
April 22, 1911

"Sues Pullman Company for Discrimination"
The Chicago Defender
May 11, 1918

The Brotherhood of Sleeping Car Porters was first organized in 1925. It was not until twelve years later that the BSCP won a collective bargaining agreement with the Pullman Company. The BSCP and its president, A. Philip Randolph, fought racial segregation throughout the United States and the South in particular up until the 1960s.

"Tipping -- An Evil"
The Chicago Defender
February 3, 1912

"Story of Struggle of Pullman Porters"
The Chicago Defender
January 5, 1929

http://www.pullman-museum.org/sleepingcars at sbcglobal.net

Nobody's Daughter

Other pictures depicting African Americans in a negative image…

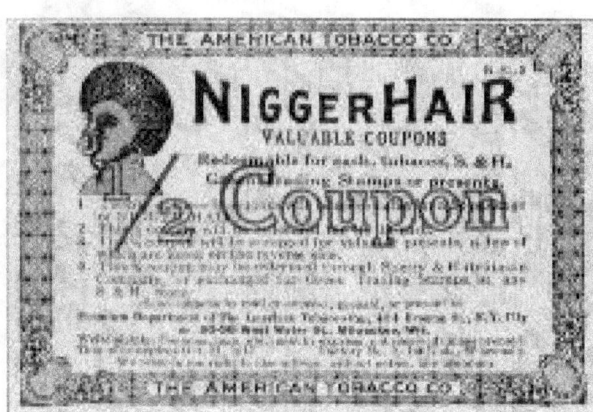

Dr. Stacey Nickleberry

Chapter 5
Grandmother Lee and My Trip to California

Grandmother Lee and Me

In the late 1890's, Grandma Lee's husband had been killed fighting in the Spanish-American War. My mother was only nine years old when a telegram came to Nana's house with the news of her dad being killed in the war. In 1949, when I was ten months old, Grandmother Lee and I went to California where her in-laws lived (my grandfather's parents). It was only befitting for my grandmother to take me to California and introduce me to my great-grandparents. Because I was only ten months old, it was an event of which I have no memory.

(Papa and Great-Grandmother)

During our visit, my great-grandparents were elated, I suppose, that I was more interested in reading the newspaper my great-grandpapa held. My great-grandfather said he was reading the newspaper while holding me on his lap, when I suddenly took the paper and climbed off his knee to the floor, placed the paper on the floor and started pretending I was reading the paper. They said I would not give them that paper until I had looked at every page.

My great-grandfather's wife Debra worked in Beverly Hills cleaning the homes of white people. She was a thief. She stole more than she was paid as the story I overheard went (the African American house help were not treated very nice or fairly). Evidently, she was good at what she did because she never got caught. Sometimes, her white employers would give her hand-me-down clothes from their children. Because of her employment, later when I was in college, I was able to wear Ralph Lauren, Jones of New York, and Letty Lee, all designers located on Michigan Ave in Chicago.

Grandma Lee was nothing like her mother Nana. Grandma Lee always seemed to have an attitude around me. It was an attitude centered with sadness. I remember seeing that look mostly every time she looked at me. I do not think Grandma Lee went to church either. I was told at an early age to not ask Grandma Lee any questions and surely not to talk sassy or even roll my eyes, anywhere near her. Children were not allowed to hear adult's conversations; that is a rule of proper upbringing. However, Nana always allowed me to ask her questions as long as the questions did not involve adult business or were considered sassing.

When I took my second trip to California to visit my great-grandparents, I was around five years old. I remember a Chinese couple who lived next door to my grandparents having a little girl my age. I had not ever seen any Chinese people before in my life. One day, I was outside playing in the front yard and my great-grandparent's neighbor brought her daughter over to meet me. They both had strange eyes. Great-Grandma Debra said I almost broke the screen door getting into the house. She asked me what was wrong. I said, "This lady and her daughter have eyes that go this way and that way." After realizing that they were just plain people like me, the little girl and I would play regularly.

From what I can remember, my great-grandparents had moved to California from the South to work on tomato farms, making twenty-five cents an hour. I could not imagine how hard the job was. However, from their labor, my great-grandfather was able to buy the property on 57th Street in Los Angeles near Slauson Ave. The property held two homes on a lot. The main house was in the front and a smaller house was in the back (it was used as a rental house and brought extra income in to assist with the mortgage payments.) This is the house my mother inherited when they both passed away, as she was the only grandchild.

Chapter 6
Walking in a Fog…Not Knowing the Reasons You Do What You Do

1 Peter 2:9- *"But ye are a chosen generation, a royal priesthood, a holy nation, a peculiar people; that ye should shew forth the praises of him who hath called you out of darkness into his marvelous light."*

    I cannot remember why it seemed I was always with Nana. However, later I was told my mom worked a lot and needed Nana to watch over me. Nana was born and raised in New Orleans, Louisiana. She had a stepsister and a stepmother. She never told me what happened to her real mother. I also never heard Nana say anything about her father either. Nana had a very light complexion and long wavy black and gray hair. She told me her mother was a Cherokee Indian. Nana left Louisiana at fifteen and married my great-grandpa.

    Nana stood 5'10" tall and did not take any mess. Nana would have been lynched had she stayed in the South.

> **3 Negroes Lynched; One a Woman, During Retrial for Murder**
>
> *Mob Storms Jail After Cutting Electric Wires and Plunging City Into Darkness Before Raid*
>
> *SEQUEL TO FATAL SHOOTING IN 1925*

I believe certain behaviors are passed down from generation to generation, because I know I could not live in any Southern city. I believe people that knew Nana would say I am a lot like her. Nana said she would never ride any bus where she had to sit in the back, after paying equal amount of fare as white people.

When Nana was a little girl, there were not any buses. People rode in buggies pulled by horses. Back then, Negroes just stayed in their place and did not bother white people, and white people kept out of their way too. I remember one mill worker who tried to slip out of paying Nana rent. I do not know where she got the gun, but it looked like the one the Lone Ranger carried. I think Nana must have kept it somewhere on her person. She must have told that man something, because all of a sudden money was flying all over the kitchen, and that man left running. I do not remember him ever coming back to get his belongings.

While I was growing up, we would often visit New Orleans during the summer months. While there, Nana's sister, my great-aunt Clara, would tell us wives' tales that scared the children to death. As most folks know, some people in New Orleans believe in witchcraft - voodoo, whatever you want to call it. My relatives on

Nobody's Daughter

Nana's side had some strange beliefs. I would hear them talking, and the things they would say were so intriguing. I would stay up listening when they thought I was asleep. Nana would scare me by telling stories about adults putting spells on other people. I remember her telling me a woman should never take her shoes off in a woman's house who is not friendly with her (especially if she is fooling around with her husband).

Aunt Clara told us this story: there was a woman who knew her husband was spending too much time at another woman's house. However, the woman always pretended to be friendly to the wife. One day, the woman had a party and invited the man and his wife. For some reason, the wife took her shoes off, and all of a sudden, her feet shriveled. Aunt Clara said, until this day, that woman never walked again, and the other lady walked off with her husband.

Dr. Stacey Nickleberry

Chapter 7
Wives' Tales from New Orleans

Rod Sterling has it right. There is a world beyond human understanding. We are fighting against good and evil. I believe these tales tried to explain the spiritual warfare as described in the Bible.

Nana told me many old wives' tales while I lived with her. I enjoyed these bedtime stories more than those children stories parents read to their children. A few stories I remember were never to give a man a watch, because it will only be a matter of time before he leaves you; never buy a man a pair of shoes because he will walk out of your life; never eat ice cream and watermelon together or eat fish and ice cream together because those combinations will kill you. Every time it rained followed by thunder and lighting, Nana said the devil was beating his wife. When it rained and the sun was shining, Nana said God was crying. Nana also said,"Never let a man come into your house on New Year's Day. You will have bad luck all year; always have money in your pocket on New Year's Eve, so you will have money all year; always take your Christmas tree down before the New Year." As a child, I believed everything Nana told me, and if any kid laughed at what Nana had told me, they were going to receive the brunt of my anger.

Remember, old folks had to have experienced those sayings or have seen someone die from eating those items together (ice cream and watermelon or fish). Negroes did not go to the doctor or a hospital back then, so when someone asked how someone had died, they usually would relate death to something that the person ate if no other reasons were available. Thus, that was the beginning of my family's Negro wives' tales.

Earlier, I mentioned Nana could see things others could not. She was born with a veil over her face (not a material veil, but something like mucus). One of the earliest marks of a psychic takes place when a child in born in the caul (also referred to as veil or hood). The caul is a thin membrane, part of the amniotic sac in which the baby grows while in the womb. A child born with a caul usually emerges with the amnion covering his or her head. It has been described as a shimmering veil. These types of births are very rare, especially today due to more interceptive birthing techniques. For the most part, being born with a caul is seen as a good omen, a sign of luck and greatness, the mark of kings (caul-bearers being born already crowned).

The caul was thought to bring wisdom, honor and truth. Cauls were often purchased by Greek and Roman statesmen. In Scandinavian tradition, the caul was associated with the presence of an accompanying spirit called a *fylgja*, which after birth would manifest as an animal, object or person. In other societies, caulbearers were believed to be impervious to drowning, as well as the cauls themselves (which can be dried and saved). Caul was highly sought after by sailors, who would buy them and often wear them in lockets as prevention against drowning. Amniomancy is a form of divination practiced by interpreting the caul. Cauls were often kept as heirlooms. Upon the death of the bearer, it was said that the caul should be burned, so its owner could rest peacefully.

Caulbearers are also said to have the ability to be able to detect underground water, to predict weather changes and to know when fish and food will be plentiful. In addition, there is the psychic ability. Born behind the veil, caulbearers are believed to possess special sensitivities, to have the ability to navigate between many worlds and to see the future. Along with the psychic gift, they are also said to be natural healers, practiced via laying on of hands or doing distance healing.

People back then (especially those in my family) believed that babies born in that condition could see the supernatural. Nana was not a fortuneteller, just a wise lady. Nana and I would walk to the store a few blocks away. All of a sudden, she would stop and say, "There goes a ghost." I thought Nana was fooling me, because I would look in the direction she pointed; however, I did not see anything, no matter how fast I looked. I asked Nana how a ghost looks. She would say, "They're about two feet tall, and they float." I asked, "Will they bother people?" She would always say, "Not if you believe in Jesus." When we had Bible study that night, I believe I was five years old. I said, "Jesus, I believe in you. Please don't turn me into no ghost." That is another story I heard repeatedly.

Dr. Stacey Nickleberry

Chapter 8
Growing Up in the Fifties in Gary, Indiana

Number running was a big business in Gary, Indiana. During the 1940's and 1950's, some people made a lot of money playing a game called "Policy." At least that is what I thought when I saw Nana counting money after the "Policy man" left. From what I saw, Nana was playing Policy numbers. I remember she would play the Green and Midnight books the most. Policy playing was an illegal activity. People in our neighborhood would play numbers they thought would come out the next day on a green slip or blue slip. The game was invented by African Americans and was similar to the lottery some people play today, which white people have made legal.

If the "Policy player" were lucky and matched the numbers for that day, the lucky player won money according to the amount of money he/she had bet that day on the Policy slip (a slip that contained numbers or one could select his/her own numbers.) Runners were men who would travel around every day to certain people to get their numbers and later that day take the winners their money when they won. Sometimes, when Nana did not have many renters in her boarding home, she played Policy.

All I remember is Nana was never broke a day in her life. I would hear her pray sometimes. She would say, "God, you know what I need, and I thank you for delivering it in the morning." Sometimes, I would run to the front door and look outside, thinking money would be on the front porch. However, around noontime, Mr. Joe, the number runner man, would knock on the door and hand Nana an envelope. I learned the envelope contained the money. Playing Policy helped Nana survive the "Great Depression," a difficult period in time for most Blacks.

Dr. Stacey Nickleberry

The Great Depression, World War II, and Beyond

As I have previously stated, my great-grandparents came from New Orleans, via Buffalo, New York from Minnesota. They survived the Great Depression, but it left visible scars that also influenced my life through Nana. Until very recently, the history of Gary remained intertwined with the fortune or folly of the steel industry. The Great Depression of the 1930s had a devastating effect on Gary's economy, especially with U.S. Steel dropping from 100 percent capacity in 1929 to 15 percent in 1932. The depression also brought unionization of Gary's industries, with U.S. Steel recognizing the Steelworkers Organizing Committee as the bargaining agent for its workers in 1937. Between 1935 and 1939, the steel worker's wages rose nationally 27 percent, benefiting Gary's workers as well.

During World War II, steel production soared, and the tide of prosperity continued for the next two decades. U.S. Steel production peaked in 1953, at more than 35 million tons. The Steelworkers Union held a series of long strikes in 1946 and 1952. These strikes were mostly nonviolent conflicts over wages and benefits rather than the bloody struggles over union recognition that happened elsewhere, but a 116-day long strike in 1959 had the world-changing effect of shutting down 90 percent of production of not only U.S. Steel, but also its competitors. This opened the door to competition from foreign steel, which had had negligible effects before. The long decline of American steel began.

Manufacturing, in general, declined in the region and in the whole country. Between 1979 and 1986, northwest Indiana's loss in manufacturing totaled 42.5 percent, largely in the areas of oil and steel. The world market changed again, and the American steel industry rebounded a bit from the late 1980s to the early 1990s. The steel industry is still important to the local economy in Gary, although it is not the world leader in steel.

Gary Works U.S. Steel was the largest manufacturing plant and was situated on the south shore of Lake Michigan. Comprised of both steelmaking and finishing facilities, Gary Works had an annual raw steelmaking capability of 7.5 million net tons. Gary

Works also operated three coke batteries, with annual production capability of 1.3 million net tons.

Sheet products, hot strip mill plate products and tin products were manufactured at Gary Works. Hot-rolled, cold-rolled and galvanized sheet products were produced for customers in the automotive, metal building components, home construction and appliance markets.

Tin mill products are used by customers in the container industry in the manufacturing of food and beverage containers, aerosol cans, paint cans and pails, and more. The plant has now gone overseas to foreign countries where wages are much lower due to exploitation of workers. The disappearance of factories along the Great Lakes has devastated the economic status and employment for many African Americans that depended on employment in these cities.

School Days

As I continued hearing my Nana's stories about our African American history and culture, I eventually began school. When Nana took me to kindergarten and left me, I thought I would be fine, for she had taught me everything I needed to know. But, later I was confused about why Nana had left me in school and amongst people I did not know. I went into shock. The teacher was very fat, smelled funny, and had the nerve to ask me if I knew the colors and the alphabet. I not only knew the colors and the alphabet, but I could read and spell all the colors.

After learning that, she told me to sit in the first seat by her desk. I knew that particular desk was for smart children, but for some reason, I took an immediate dislike to her. By noontime, I was very bored. I told the teacher, "Okay, I have learned enough for one day. Nana said I could go home." That was the first day of school and my first spanking of many in a school. When I got home and told Nana what that teacher did, she said, "You know better than to tell a lie, Stacey. You know how much I hate lying." To this day, I cannot stand a liar, either.

Early in life, I knew I had the gift to teach. Every opportunity was a moment for me to teach. I would make the neighborhood children sit on my neighbor's stairs, where my friends and I would play school. I would ask them an easy question and pretend if they answered the questions correctly, they were moved to the next grade. As they moved up the stairs, the questions became harder. I educated many children in my neighborhood. We were easily entertained back then. We would create our own games; mostly, we played house and school.

The United States Open Door Foreigners Policy

During the late 1940's, people from Czechoslovakia and Yugoslavia were migrating to Gary, Indiana because of the Steel Mills. Gary, Indiana is located very close to Lake Michigan. The location made it easy for ships to move in and out and pick up steel from the mill. Nana became friendly with a Czechoslovakian woman who lived across the street. Nana would iron for her, and she taught Nana how to make Sauerkraut and sausage, a common Czechoslovakian dish. Nana made that meal every Sunday for a couple of months. I hated it, even to this day! The Negro children and the Czechoslovakian children played together without any problems. But, by the time my Czechoslovakian girlfriends reached adolescence, they had moved from our neighborhood. I heard adults say the Czechoslovakians moved away because they did not want their girls marrying Negro boys.

With the conclusion of World War II, Indiana rebounded to levels of production prior to the Great Depression. The Steel Industry became the primary employer, a trend that continued into the 1960s. Urbanization during the 1950s and 1960s led to substantial growth in the state's cities. The auto, steel and pharmaceutical industries topped Indiana's major businesses. Indiana's population continued to grow during the years after the war, exceeding five million by the 1970 census. In the 1960s, the administration of Matthew E. Welsh adopted its first sales tax of two percent. Indiana schools were desegregated in 1949. In 1950, the Census Bureau reported Indiana's population as 95.5% white and 4.4% black. Governor Welsh also worked with the General Assembly to pass the Indiana Civil Rights Bill, granting equal protection to minorities in seeking employment.

Originally an agricultural state, Indiana was settled by Native Americans moving west, by a small group of French Creoles and European immigrant farmers. Although railroad building and industrialization attracted other immigrant groups—notably the Irish, Hungarians, Italians, Poles, Croats, Slovaks, and Syrians—foreign immigration to Indiana declined sharply in the 20th century, although there was a rebound in the final decade. As of 2000, foreign-born Hoosiers numbered 186,534 (3% of the total state population), nearly double the figure of 94,263 in 1990. Restrictions on foreign immigration and the availability of jobs spurred the migration of black Americans to Indiana after World War I; by 2000, the state had 510,034 blacks, representing about 8.4% of the total population. Approximately one-fifth of all Indiana blacks live in the industrial city of Gary. In 2004, 8.8% of the population was black.

Chapter 9
A Change in My Environment

I do not know what happened, but my mother came and took me away from Nana. All of a sudden, I had a little sister and a baby brother. I remember we lived upstairs over a gas station. She told me, "I will be working downstairs," and in the same breath, she said, "You have a new father." I was wondering what happened to the old father. This new father's complexion was very light, and he had curly jet-black hair and a big stomach. He laughed a lot, and immediately, I liked him. I did not know what to think of this sister and brother thing, and I did not have Nana to ask. My baby brother was ten months old when I met him. He also had thick black curly hair. I do not know why my mother cut his hair before he was a year old, and I tell you, his hair never was curly again. Nana had told me you are not supposed to cut a baby's hair before he or she reaches a year old. I told my mother what Nana had said, but she did not listen.

Down the hall from our upstairs apartment lived two women. They were sisters, and they would babysit for my mother, even though my mother worked in the office downstairs. One day in particular, my mother had left my brother's stroller in the hallway. I always carried my baby brother even though he was fat and heavy for me. On that particular day, I wanted to take my baby brother downstairs, so my sister and I placed him in the stroller and thought we could roll him down two flights of stairs by ourselves. Somehow, I lost my grip on the stroller and down the stairs my baby brother went. He laughed all the way down the stairs and luckily for me the door was closed. Otherwise, he would have kept rolling across Broadway, one of the major streets in our little town.

They do not make strollers the way they used too. That stroller kept the baby inside, and it did not flip over. My baby brother did not have a scratch. However, my mother heard all the commotion and saw her baby in the stroller at the bottom of the stairs; I received the worst spanking in my life, the second of many!

That incident was the first of my many shenanigans. I was very smart for my age and for some reason, I decided to go outside on top of our roof. My mother was not the type that went outside to watch me as I played. So, I was outside alone. On that particular day, there was a chair near the clothesline. I thought I could swing on the clothesline, but I needed the chair to reach it. I climbed on the chair and placed the clothesline around my neck, and then the chair fell out from under me. I would have hung myself if my dad had not come out looking for me. He saved my life. I knew then that God had a plan for my life.

My dad treated me like his own. He always introduced me as his oldest daughter. He was the fifth born of thirteen children. His family lived in Mississippi. His father was Scottish, and his mother was part Cherokee Indian, just like Nana. His name was Dan. Dan had also moved to Gary because of the steel mills. He immediately got a job and met my mother. Knowing my dad, he probably told my mother to go and get me, which contributed to the fact I was not with Nana anymore. Luckily for me, we did not live too far from Nana. My mother knew I was very smart, so one day she walked me to Nana's house. From then on, every time I had a chance, I would go see Nana.

My new dad was always a happy person, and he could cook better than my mother could. When my mother came home, he had dinner ready. (He worked the 4 to 12 shift.) The only thing I heard my mother say about my dad's cooking was 'he cooked all the food up.'

As far as his family was concerned, he had two brothers living in Gary. One brother repaired televisions and radios, and the other sold Ford cars. His other brothers and a sister lived in Ohio, while his other sisters lived in the South and still live there to this day.

Chapter 10
My First Trip to New Orleans

I was approximately five years old when Grandma Lee took me on the City of New Orleans Train, which left from the Chicago Station. It was a long ride, and I was scared of Grandma Lee. Finally, I mustered up enough nerve to ask her when we were going to get there. She said, "In a little while." I said, "Evidently, your watch is broken because it has passed a little while." (To this day, I know somebody else said that and not me.) The next thing I remember was getting up off the center aisle of the train. I never asked Grandma Lee another question.

When we stopped in Mississippi, I could see from the window an ice cream stand with two windows. One said 'white's only,' and the other said 'colored only.' I wondered what 'colored' meant. I knew how to color, but I did not know I was colored. I did not know at the time the meaning of the word 'nigger' or that it referred to Grandma Lee and me. I was going to ask Nana when I got home about the word 'nigger.'

Many people got off the train at a rest stop and got in the line for niggers, but not Grandma Lee. I guess she figured out that I wanted to know why. She said, "I will never step foot on any Mississippi soil another day of my life." Again, that was another question I had to ask Nana when I got home. I was so happy I had my Nana who explained things to me.

Dr. Stacey Nickleberry

As a little girl, I was extremely protected from the realities of the real world. I believe we were protected from the harshness of the pictures above because my mother knew her children would rise above all forms of discrimination. She believed what the Bible says in Isaiah 54:17, *"No weapon formed against her children would prosper."* I believe my ancestors wanted us to have a wholesome childhood. However, unbeknownst to them, shielding us from the ugly world and how white people treated Negroes differently caused unforeseen pain.

One of my childhood's happiest moments occurred while visiting my cousins who lived in New Orleans. I was younger than my cousins and for the first time, I was considered the baby. My aunt Clara had warned my cousins not to take me near the creek. One day, we were walking and not really paying attention to where we were, and all of a sudden, I heard my cousin say, "Run!" As I started running, I turned around and a huge gator was coming faster than lightening. I must have run out of shock because my little feet kicked into gear. I beat both my cousins back to the house. When I was able (after catching my breath) to tell what happened, my cousins got a good spanking. They were angry for a long time with me for telling. They would not let me swing from the pecan trees anymore, which was the only form of recreation in the bayou. They were dumb. They could not read nor write, but they were older than I. Furthermore, they would not allow me teach them.

Purple and Gold Beads

1872 was the year that a group of businessmen invented a King of Carnival--Rex--to preside over the first daytime parade. Honoring visiting Russian Grand Duke Alexis Romanoff, they introduced his family colors of purple, green, and gold as Carnival's official colors. Purple stands for justice; gold for power; and green for faith. This was also the Mardi Gras season that Carnival's improbable anthem, "If Ever I Cease to Love," was cemented, due in part to the Duke's fondness for the tune.

In 1873, floats began to be entirely constructed in New Orleans instead of France, culminating with Comus' magnificent "The Missing Links to Darwin's Origin of Species," in which exotic paper-mache' animal costumes served as the basis for Comus to mock both Darwin's theory and local officials, including Governor

Nobody's Daughter

Henry Warmoth. In 1875, Governor Warmoth signed the "Mardi Gras Act," making Fat Tuesday a legal holiday in Louisiana, which it still is (www.mardigrasneworleans.com/history.html).

Despite the holiday's rich history in New Orleans, Louisiana, Mayor Sam Jones of Mobile, Alabama, says the first Mardi Gras celebration in this country actually took place in his city, and most Mobile natives agree.

I remember another time going to New Orleans with Grandma Lee. She took me to the Mardi Gras. The people on the floats were dressed in costumes with pretty colors, and float riders wore mask. They would throw green and purple beads from the floats, into the crowds of people along the side streets. They hardly ever threw beads to the Negro people. However, Grandma Lee was tall and could jump. She would watch the direction the hand was going to throw the beads and jump right in front of the white people and grab the beads almost right from their hands. By the time the parade was over, Grandma Lee must have had a hundred beads. I thought those beads were money the way people were fighting to catch them. Therefore, I was cheering for Grandma Lee to get the beads and would be overjoyed when she out jumped the white people. I never liked the Mardi Gras parades. I did not care to see Grandma Lee jumping to get those beads that I never liked.

However, one thing I did love about New Orleans was the pecan trees in my Aunt Clara's yard. Aunt Clara had several pecan trees in her yard. Every year, she would send Grandma Lee pecans, so she could make pecan pies for Thanksgiving and Christmas. Grandma Lee could make pecan pies well, but I sure hated her fruitcakes. Fruitcakes just had too much stuff in them. It should have been called "Junk Cake."

Down in the bayou of New Orleans, it is very scary at night. It is so dark one cannot see his/her hand in front of his/her face. If you had to use the bathroom back in those days, the toilet was outside. It was called 'the outhouse.' The outhouse had a dirt floor and was not a real toilet.

I was scared to go outside to the 'outhouse,' especially at night. Grandma got so tired of me wetting the bed because I refused to use the outhouse. It was bad enough going in there during daylight. Eventually, Grandma Lee let me use a bedpan.

We also attended church in New Orleans.

Nobody's Daughter

In New Orleans, when folks would leave a neighbor's home, they would always say, "I'll see you later if the creeks don't rise." I asked my aunt Clara what was meant by 'if the creek does not rise.' She explained New Orleans sat below sea level, and if the Mississippi River, which New Orleans' residents referred to as the creek, would ever rise above the levees, New Orleans would be completely submerged in water deeper than the tallest trees and a devastating flood would occur. I heard this saying as a little girl as early as I can remember, around the age of five and continued to hear, "If the creek don't rise!" People who do not know anything about New Orleans would ask, "Why didn't the people of New Orleans leave before Hurricane Katrina?" There were always hurricanes, some severe and some not so severe, but the creek had never risen. The people who governed the city had always assured everyone that the levees would hold a hurricane level 6. Hurricane Katrina was a level 6.

New Orleans, Louisiana after Hurricane Katrina

Dr. Stacey Nickleberry

Chapter 11
Not Only My Heritage, but also My Cultural Experiences

Arriving home from New Orleans and seeing Nana, I had many questions. Nana told me Grandma Lee's first husband was killed for stealing chickens by the Ku Klux Klan. She said, "They dragged him out of his parent's house, cut him up real bad and hung him on a big tree branch." He was twenty years old at the time. Nana said, "Nobody did anything about it." She said, "Grandma Lee ran away to New York to live with some relatives." These were devastating stories I heard and read about in newspapers. I always wonder how white people could be so cruel and still say they were human beings. Some folks were just blinded to the facts.

Dr. Stacey Nickleberry

The Ku Klux Klan

I was always told that Indiana was the headquarters for the Ku Klux Klan, who was also referred to as "White Supremacists." "Founded in 1866, the Ku Klux Klan (KKK) extended into almost every southern state by 1870 and became a vehicle for white southern resistance to the Republican Party's Reconstruction Era policies aimed at establishing political and economic equality for blacks. Its members waged an underground campaign of intimidation and violence directed at white and black Republican leaders" (blacksphere.net/2013/06/civil-wrongs-the-ku-klux-klan).

Growing up in Gary, Indiana, I never noticed racism until my mother would take us shopping downtown. I did notice the difference in the treatment my mother received compared to white people. I never understood the reason salespersons followed us around the store.

Chapter 12
Gaining Spiritual Insight in Church

Proverbs 9:10- *"The fear of the Lord is the beginning of wisdom and the knowledge of the holy is understanding."*

I have always been in church as long as I can remember. Every Sunday, I was in church. Nana's Baptist church had strange beliefs. (The church was probably a Holy-Roller Church. I just do not remember). I do remember the women wore long skirts and blouses that covered everything. They wore very little make-up, if any at all. Women who attended Nana's church could not wear anything red, and the mothers of the church were always looking around staring at people.

Sometimes, I hated going to church, because the mothers of the church would always say I was in "self." "Self" meant one had a proud look and had too much pride. That was a big sin to them back then. I had to sit on the "sinner's bench." I did not mind sitting on the sinner's bench because I was just that determined to never let anyone see me "sweat" or think they had hit a nerve. (I am still that way to this day. Unless you really get on my nerves you will never be able to know when I am upset).

It was not until I had a special encounter with the Lord that I understood that church experience. I heard Grandma Lee did not like church because she felt that ministers were ungodly. I heard her say that the reverend would have the women cook him Sunday dinner even if the husbands objected, which explained why I saw more women in church than men, during my upbringing.

Dr. Stacey Nickleberry

Chapter 13
Life with the Only Dad I Knew

My stepfather raised three children: me, my sister, and my brother. I believe I was around seven when my mother developed tuberculosis and was rushed to the hospital. My dad, my siblings, and I moved with Nana. It was more convenient for the family because Nana could babysit while my dad worked. She had plenty of room, so it must have been the best choice for my family at the time. My mother survived the ordeal because Nana prayed so hard and long every night while she was in the hospital.

Nana used to pray so hard she would be soaking wet the next morning when I went into her bedroom, and she would still be on her knees. Nana was a "prayer warrior." If she prayed about something, it surely happened. My mother inherited that gift. I believed my mother could raise the dead. When my mother prayed, you had better hope you had not done anything against her to get on her bad side. I believed my mother could kill people with her prayers. Maybe that should be a story for my next book.

It took awhile before my mother could come home from the hospital. However, when she got her strength back, we moved away from Nana, again. Around that time, we moved to Rhode Island Street, not too far from my favorite cousin Michael Gregory, who is presently retired from the position of Gary, Indiana Fire Department Chief Inspector.

My dad with my sister (left) and me (right)

Dr. Stacey Nickleberry

My Relationship with my Mother

Proverbs 31:10-13- *"A capable, intelligent, and Virtuous woman who is he who can find her? She is far more precious than jewels and her value is far above rubies or pearls. The heart of her husband trusts in her confidently, relies on, and believes in her securely, so that he has no lack of {honest} gain or need of {dishonest} spoil. She comforts, encourages, and does him only good as long as there is life within her. She seeks out wool and flax and works with willing hands {to develop it}."*

My mother

My mother never liked confusion, so she would always say, "Why live in hell and go to hell too?" I will contribute her statement to the fact she came so close to leaving this earth at a very young age. One night, when we lived upstairs over a gas station, I heard my mother fussing with my dad about drinking too much. I was too young to know the brand of liquor he drank, but I remember my mother making a clock and using the liquor tops as the spokes around the clock, and each bottle top, that looked like a spoke had at least six or seven liquor tops. That man drank a lot. I believe my mother had grown tired of getting him out of the bars late at night. He worked the 4-12 midnight shifts mostly, but I think he was messing up his job at the steel mill.

When my dad finally left his family, my mother had no problem finding a replacement. My mother is a pretty ebony complexion and was tall and slim with big legs and a nice personality. My mother was nothing like her mother or grandmother; her personality was probably inherited from her father's side of the family.

When I was younger, she tried to spank the hell out of me, but it just did not work. To add to my spankings was old Mrs. Evans who lived next door; I believe she was the neighborhood spy.

When my mother was not spanking us, she was raising us to be responsible. She instilled in my sister and me the importance of being women and how to dress appropriately. I was the oldest, so learning how to clean, cook, wash, and protect my siblings, no matter what, were my duties. My number one responsibility was to make sure no one hurt them. My mother worked three jobs, and she made sure we were well kept and wore the best clothes. All the clothes she did not buy were sent from the children of the rich white families for whom my great-grandmother Debra worked. Many of the clothes still had the price tags.

I believe we were good children back then. I respected my mother. She could just give me a look when I had gone a little too far with my behavior or attitude. My sister was the best child. She never gave my mother one ounce of trouble. I believe, as I got older, I became too much for her to handle. I was opinionated and stubborn. I was going to have my way by any means necessary. If my mother said, "Go right," I went left. If she said, "The sky is blue," I would say, "It is purple."

In raising her children, mother followed the traditions she was taught. We had to be in the house *before* the street lights came on. Sometimes, we attended church all day on Sundays. We ate dinner by 2:00pm., and everybody ate in the dining room together. Homework was left on the table every night, so my mother could check it. Saturday was for cleaning, washing, ironing, and cooking dinner for Sunday. No one played outside on Sundays; however, when we became older, Sunday was movie day, if we went to church first.

My mother taught us the best she knew because she wanted a happy life for her children. She gave my sister and me the mother-to-daughter talk early. She talked to us about early pregnancy. She made an extra point by encouraging us to get an education, mainly because she got pregnant before getting her college degree.

I hated those conversations because I really liked boys, but my mother had told me kissing would lead to me having a baby, and then my life would be ruined. I believed my mom. And one thing I really did not want to do was to shame my family. Another thing I observed was how hard my mother worked. I was determined at an early age I was not going to work that hard for anyone. My mother did an excellent job in bringing up children in the way they should go and when they are old, they will not depart from it. This statement is directly from the Bible.

As she raised us, my mother told us about how she grew up. She told us about when she was in elementary school. The Negro schools received the hand-me-down books from the white schools, even though the schools were in the same district. Because the white schools knew that the old books were going to the Negro schools, they would draw pictures of Negroes being hung in trees or they would write Black Sambo or nigger throughout the books. Money was scarce in the Negro schools, and they could not afford to buy new books. The teachers tried to screen the books, but some of the books were passed through the system undetected, and Negro children had to use those books with those awful pictures and words.

The images my mom grew up observing made it more important to me to try my best to make her proud. I understand now why she was so hard on us. Thank you, Mommy Betty Ann.

My mother thought as most Black people did when John F. Kennedy was elected president. They thought things were going to change in America for us. Calling ourselves Negroes mostly was discontinued, and we began calling ourselves Black, during the mid-sixties. I contribute some of this to the Black Panthers and other Black Power Movements, Minister Malcolm X and singer James Brown's song, "I'm Black and I'm Proud."

James Brown

Fans and admirers refer to him, commonly and without hyperbole, as "the Godfather of Soul," "Soul Brother Number One" and "the hardest working man in show business." Michael Jackson cited him as "my greatest inspiration." And the critic Robert Christgau, writing in *Rolling Stone*, called him "the greatest musician of the rock era, no contest." With some 800 songs in his repertoire, James Brown has influenced contemporary artists from virtually every popular music genre - rock, soul, jazz, R&B. His polyrhythmic funk vamps virtually reshaped dance music, and his impact on hip-hop, in particular, was huge; in the music's early years, Brown was by far the most sampled artist (http://www.rollingstone.com/music/artists/jamesbrown/biography#ixzz2fDGeKyMO).

The Jackson Five, walking down Broadway, Gary, Indiana

Chapter 14
Why Don't I Have My Own Father?

By the time I was in fifth grade, enrolled in Dunbar-Pulaski school, I remember wondering about the whereabouts of my biological father. I finally met him at the age of ten. He and I did not resemble one another facially. I understand why he had been missing in action, not coming around his oldest daughter, me: He had another family.

I remember calling my father regularly and asking to be with him. He would promise every Sunday after church he would come, but he never did. I would sit by the window waiting for him to show up until nighttime, and mother would make me go to bed. I felt abandoned, although it was not a term I understood. However, as a little girl, seeing other girls my age with a father did not sit well with me.

I believe every little girl needs a father who is caring and loving. It is God's purpose for this to occur. God knew what He was doing when He placed Adam and Eve in the garden. We humans are the ones who went in our own misguided way.

I do not remember ever meeting many of my biological father's family. Finally, in high school, I met two of my paternal cousins, and we became close (Marie and Bennie Simmons). Other family I did meet looked and behaved strangely around me. I realize now part of the reason was this one fact: I possessed none of their facial features. My father's mother, in my opinion, frequently seemed to have an attitude every time I visited, which she tried hard to hide. My grandfather on my biological father's side was very nice to me. Every Christmas Eve he would come by my mother's house and give me two dollars. I now know why my mother rolled her eyes every time I showed her what he had given me. My mother being a Christian woman in front of her children never said to him what her rolling her eyes told me.

Chapter 15
My Elementary and Junior High Era

I remember attending Pulaski Elementary and Junior High School. In the late 50's, we remained in the same school from kindergarten to ninth grade. I remember my fifth grade teachers the most. Mrs. Bryant taught English; Jean Gillespie (my aunt) taught mathematics; and Ms. Cope taught drama. I cannot remember my social studies teacher's name; however, I appreciate her because I grew to love social studies, the subject I taught when I became a teacher. She made us memorize the "Gettysburg Address," in the fifth grade. I knew more in fifth grade than kids graduating from high school in California. During that era, teachers taught and meant business.

Coach Dennis taught math and physical education. I believe he was my fourth grade math teacher. He was one teacher who meant business, and no one talked in his class unless he gave permission. Mrs. Gillespie, my aunt, was too nice and very pretty. She was a lovely teacher who encouraged us to perform at our best. She did not swat students. I remember she would always wink when her students got a problem correct, and she made learning interesting.

In Coach Dennis' class, I remember receiving a swat every time I missed 9x8. Coach Dennis would make you forget your mama's name. He was very strict. All the students were scared to death of him in my class. Every day before taking attendance, Mr. Dennis would start with each row of desks. There were six rows of desks and six students per row. He would go up and down each row asking each student a different times table. Sometimes, he would ask me an easy one, but most of the time I would get 9x8 and a swat. For the life of me, I could not remember 9x8 = 72. I have a phobia today concerning 9x8.

In fifth grade, we had some fast girls who had boyfriends and played "house" during lunch break. I do not know how a fight between Helen and me started. I know she was told to fight me, probably over a boy who liked me and not her (she played with those fast girls.) She came up to me and said she wanted to fight.

Before she could get the word 'fight' out of her mouth, I popped her on the head with my lunch pail. (Lunch pails were made a lot stronger than they are today. Believe me! It might have been steel.) Blood went everywhere. It really scared me, because she fell to the ground, with blood all over her face. Immediately, the teachers dragged me kicking and fighting all the way to the principal's office. (I thought they were taking me to jail because I had killed Helen.) My mother was called on her job, and I was suspended for fighting. Helen was okay! She was struck on the soft part of her eyebrow, and she did not get stitches. (She probably has that scar today over her eye. Poor child.)

Chapter 16
Summertime

During the summer, we always took trips. We did not stay home the entire summer. We travelled to Ohio, where my dad's family lived. I really enjoyed visiting my cousins Barbara and Lawrence and my Uncle Junior. During one particular trip, we finally stopped at a gas station. I never will forget. It was in a small town in Missouri before we crossed the bridge. (Back then, there were not any roads like there are today. (You also had to travel through towns to get down South.)

There were some white men standing in front of the gas station wearing overalls and another white man was pumping gas. My dad said to the white man pumping gas, "Do you sell pop?' (People from the mid-west states call soda'pop'! I guess my dad's question gave them a clue we were not from around there). The man spun around and looked at the new yellow 54 or 57 model T-Bird and said, "We don't serve niggers."

Without one word, my dad slowly pulled out of the gas station. It was miles before I heard my dad say, "It's going to come a day it will not matter what your skin color is. You are going to be treated with respect."

We lived on Connecticut Street in Gary. There must have been thirty kids my age on the block. One summer, we were playing baseball in the vacant lot in the middle of the block, when Thomas, the "Special Need" kid, wanted to play with us. Everybody said, "No!" Usually, he would just sit and watch. However, on that particular day, I guess "no" was the wrong answer. When the batter dropped the bat and began running the bases, Thomas picked up the bat and began chasing everyone near him with the bat. Thomas must have hit a few kids that could not run fast enough to get out his way. The next time we played baseball and Thomas asked to play, you had better believe we let him play.

Sometimes, we would play cricket with beer cans and a stick. We had the most fun in the summer, playing games that we made up along the way. On our block, there were a few apartment buildings mixed in with residential homes. The apartment across from my house had many children, and their parents must have been very poor, but at that time, I did not know what poor was.

I only remember my mother making peanut butter and jelly sandwiches, and those kids would know when we ate lunch and they were right there, so my mother always made extra to give to our friends. As we grew older, I guess my family's kindness was forgotten, because all the kids across the street would try to fight my sister. My sister was nothing like me. Phyllis was scared of her own shadow when we were growing up. I guess she was just mild-mannered. I, on the other hand, would fight at the drop of a hat.

I do not care what anyone said about my sister. If they laid hands on her while I was out of sight, I asked no questions when I met up with the person who had the nerve to touch my sister. Boy, did they get beat up! I was the same towards my baby brother. We called him Danny Boy. No one bothered them afterwards because they knew I would take care of them. It would not matter if they were bigger than I was. It seemed as if I was always fighting somebody. Most of the time, I tried to be nice to most kids on the block as long as they kept their hands off my sister, my brother, and me.

While living on Connecticut Street, my mother made my sister and me take piano lessons, hoping I would use my hands for something other than fighting. My piano teacher was strict and expected her students to practice before the next session. That was impossible because we did not have a piano at home. She would wrack my knuckles with a ruler every time I missed a note. When I finished piano lessons with her, I had to soak my hands in alcohol. My mother decided music was not in our future. I think she felt bad because she could not afford to buy us a piano. (Thank you, Mrs. Alsobrooks.) Even though I can't play a piano you taught me determination.

Nosey Neighbors

Between the ages of 12-14 years of age, I lived in a neighborhood where every adult could whip my behind. I believe every neighborhood had one parent who took the responsibility for policing the children whose parents worked. Our neighborhood's "Watch Person" was Mrs. Evans. That lady was always peeping out her front window or pretending to be sweeping her front sidewalk. Everyday, my mother would walk home from one of her day jobs. The moment my mother walked into the house, Mrs. Evans was on the phone telling her about the boys I was talking to, how I left the neighborhood block, instead of staying on my porch like my mother had told me, etc!

I knew I was going to get a whipping, so I would always hand my mother the belt as soon as she got off the phone with Mrs. Evans. During the late 50's and early 60's parents did not listen to their children. Whatever an adult said about the children became fact. In addition, the children did not dare to call a grown person a liar, not if they wanted to live and have a long life. Every adult who knew a child and his/her parents and observed the child doing something wrong could spank him/her on the spot, with no questions asked. In addition, when the child told his/her parents what happened, he/she received another spanking. I learned early, one whipping a day was enough! In addition, when the pastor of our church found out, he will put you on the sinner's bench. So, as I got older, I was not always alone, there were many children sinning.

In the summertime on Connecticut Street, most children were trained to come inside when the streetlights came on. If the streetlight came on and you were not in front of your house or coming through the door, your mother would call your name so loudly, it could be heard in the next city. I hated when my mother would call my name in public, so I made every effort to be near the house, so she could at least see I was coming home.

My girlfriend in junior high school was Lottie. She and I were only friends at school because she lived in the opposite direction of my house, and it was too far to visit her outside of school. Lottie and I received the worst swatting from Mrs. Williams, our physical education (PE) coach, for skating on soap in the shower. I do not know what we were thinking; we probably were not thinking at all.

For PE classes, a curtain was used to separate the girls' PE class from the boys' PE class. When we had co-ed activities, the curtain was pulled back. For example, we had to dance with those stinky boys during the spring time, because it was part of the PE curriculum. The dance was 'square dancing.' Pulaski Junior High School boys had two left feet. My situation did not help the dancing either. I was dyslexic when it came to turning left or right. As I grew older, I found ways to overcome that impaired ability. To decrease my impairment when dancing, I always chose a partner who could at least turn in the right directions.

Besides having to square dance with the boys, school was very nerve wrecking. Teachers would embarrass us in front of our peers. The worst thing in those days was for a teacher to criticize us in public. Back then, teachers called it as they saw it. If we were dumb or stupid, that is what we were called. (Teachers scared us into shape.) Some teachers were a little politer in high school though. My English teacher would say, "Did you leave your brains under the bed?" especially if she asked you a question that you really should have known the correct answer. Most of the time, she really got on the basketball players, who were good on the basketball court but not so bright in the classroom.

As time passed, I entered the ninth grade. I finally considered myself having a boyfriend named Poochie. He was very shy or at least was pretending to be. We both just settled for liking each other and that was about it. I would get the worst whippings for going over to his house. My mother did not like Poochie. But I was just happy knowing he was my boyfriend, even without us discussing our relationship. He was the first boy that I really let kiss me; however, we were both too afraid to go any further. At least that is what I thought then. It was not until high school that I "REALLY" began to like the opposite sex. I am not implying I went all the way in high school as it was referred. I was too afraid of what my parents would think. I never wanted to disrespect my mother. I believed then refraining from sex was an unwritten law or something. Sex was never discussed among my friends. I guess it was always understood sex was something we were not to engage in.

My generation is called the "Baby Boomers." Here is a little information about us that also contributed to my attitude: We were born between 1946 and 1964. Baby Boomers are predominately in their 50s and early and late 60s. We are well established in our careers and hold positions of power and authority. This segment of the population constitutes a large majority of today's law firm leaders, corporate executives, senior paralegals and legal managers. In fact, nearly 70 percent of law firm partners are Baby Boomers.

Baby Boomers are extremely hard-workers and motivated by position, perks and prestige. Baby Boomers relish long workweeks and define themselves by their professional accomplishments. Baby Boomers sacrificed a great deal to get where they are in their career. This workaholic generation believes that Generation X and Generation Y should pay their dues and conform to a culture of overwork. Baby Boomers may criticize younger generations for a lack of work ethic and commitment to the workplace. Baby Boomers are confident, independent, and self-reliant. Baby Boomers' generation grew up in an era of reform and believes they can change the world. They questioned established authority systems and challenged the status quo.

In the legal workplace, Baby Boomers are not afraid of confrontation and will not hesitate to challenge. With increased educational and financial opportunities than previous generations, Baby Boomers are achievement-oriented, dedicated and career-focused. They welcome exciting, challenging projects and strive to make a difference.

Since Baby Boomers equate work and position with self-worth, they are quite competitive in the workplace. They are clever, resourceful and strive to win. Boomers believe in hierarchal structure and rankism and may have a hard time adjusting to workplace flexibility trends. They believe in "face time" at the office and may fault younger generations for working remotely.

Chapter 17
And Suddenly No Father

I never witnessed my mother falling apart even when she and my stepdad went their separate ways. What transpired between my mom and dad was never openly discussed as adults never spoke about divorce. I had to look the word up to understand the meaning. You would not have known around the time that my stepfather and mother had divorced.

But, it would have helped me see her being venerable, because it may have assisted me in being softer in my temperament in my later years. Knowing to express hurt and disappoint is not shameful. We were not ever able to hear or discuss adult business. All I knew was my mother continued to work.

Life was hard for my mother after she divorced my stepfather. Nana said that yellow T-Bird went to his head. Women were chasing him all over town, and she assumed that one of those "fast-tail women" fooled him, by telling him she had a lot of money somewhere out west. (I heard an adult conversation one night when I was supposed to have been asleep.) My stepfather acted just like a man who thought with his private part and not his head. He went chasing after a lie. That is what Nana said, and I had no idea what she meant, but I knew I could not ask her anything about that because it may have sounded too grown up to ask, and children were told to stay in a child's place.

My mother is to be respected and applauded for raising three children. All three of her children were teenagers at the time and raising them was not an easy task. My mom, a strong woman of faith, was able to save enough money and move us into a house. Looking back on that period of time, I knew she could have just thrown in the towel and quit; however, she did not. Thank you, Mom, for being a strong role model who definitely gave me the strength to becoming the woman I am today. As a mother, my mother's example is what held me together through all of my "life storms." I was fortunate to have a strong female role model. However, at the same time during that period of my life, I also wanted a father. I needed a male role model in my life. Later, you will realize the reason why.

Chapter 18
High School Days

God works in mysterious ways. My biological father was the Boiler Engineer for my high school. I just knew that would be the perfect time for him to try and have a father/daughter relationship with me. But that was wishful thinking. However, I developed a close relationship with his only sister's children, my cousins, rather than with him. Therefore, by the time I was a teenager, I cared less about my "biological so-called father" and his strange family. During my teenage years, I really had a bad attitude, and some called it terrible. I was always fighting; I fought with both boys and girls. It did not matter. In reality, I was angry at the lack of attention I received while growing up from my father and his family. Lacking my father's presence caused me to have anger issues as a teenager.

Despite my anger issues and the fights I was involved in, I loved high school. In Gary, there were only two high schools that I prefer to mention: Roosevelt High School and Froebel High School. Being rebellious, I chose to attend the rival school of both my parents and relatives: Froebel High. My high school was located on 15th Avenue. The Blue Devil was our school mascot and I was so proud to be a "Blue Devil."

My high school: Froebel High School Gary, Indiana

At school, I met many awesome teachers. I remember Ms. Todd, my PE Teacher, who insisted I swim across the entire pool. I told her I could not. She threw me in, and it was swim or drown. Because I am still here today, you can guess I swam.

In high school, I was very popular because I dressed in the latest styles. At that time, girls wore straight skirts with a kick pleat in the back, English Knit sweaters, and Jacqueline shoes. I wore the Aretha Franklin hair cut with a lot of hair at the top and cut short of the sides and back. It looked a little like the 'Rihanna look' of today. I also had a coke-cola bottle shape, with big legs and a small waistline. If I must say, I was one fine young woman.

My high school sweetheart was the captain of the football team. He was tall, dark, and handsome. I had no idea what love was. I just liked boys and the more the merrier. I had boyfriends all over the place; I had a black book unknown to any of my many boyfriends. I had more boyfriends than girlfriends. I disliked silly girls, and because I did not take any mess, most girls stayed away from me because back then if you looked like you wanted some of me, you got socked in the mouth.

I remember some girls from Roosevelt High School came to Froebel to take summer classes. My school and Roosevelt High School were rival schools. Us Froebel girls thought they were there to take our boyfriends. (I must add Froebel High School had the better-looking young men.) Therefore, everybody was talking and trying to figure out how the Froebel girls should handle this blatant disrespect. As a result, the hurricane in me rose up, and I went up to one of the Roosevelt chicks. I said, "Hey, why are you here?" She had the nerve to roll her eyes at me, and before I knew it, I had grabbed her by her ponytail and had her on the ground whaling the mess out of her. They said, "All of a sudden, everybody was fighting." Girls' blouses were torn off; hair was pulled; and there was biting. It was a total mess. By the time the city police arrived, the Froebel girls had chased those Roosevelt girls back across the railroad tracks.

Nobody's Daughter

That evening, my mother got a phone call from Dr. James, the principal, to come to his office to discuss my behavior. Because I had started the fight, I was kicked out of summer school. My mother was mad! She had always told me not to start a fight but to finish one. So for the rest of the summer, I had to stay with Nana, to help her with the boarding house. That was the best summer of my life.

The Lessons I Learned from my Mother

My mother was not an angry type of woman; she was not one to say all white people were devils. In fact, my mother helped many white people. She did not care what skin color a person possessed. If they needed something and she had it, she would give it to them, with no questions asked. In that way, I am a lot like my mother. I am always giving something away. I enjoy helping people. If someone asks me for something, and I have it, I give it.

Although my mother was kindhearted, she disliked this one thing: throwing your clothes or coats over chairs or on the bed. She had warned me many of times to hang my coat up when I arrived home from school. One day, I went to put my coat on and could not find it anywhere in the house. I asked my mother if she had seen my coat. She said, "Yes." I asked, "Then where it is?" She said, "In the alley in the trash can." I could not believe my mother had thrown my black leather coat in the trashcan, but there it was in the trashcan. From that day, until I got my own place, I hung up all my clothes.

My mother also kept up with what we wore a lot and what we did not use. I was a roller skating fool back in the day, but when I went away to college, I really did not skate that often. One day, I decided I was going to go skating, so I went to my closet to look for my skates. It took me by surprise that my mother had given my skates away. When I got older, I used to tease her by saying, "If it was not nailed down, Miss Ann is going to find someone who needed it!"

In my later years, I learned my mother was often taken advantage of because of her kind heart. Negro women in Gary were treacherous. My mother would say, "Never tell the left hand what the right hand is doing." As I got older, I found myself telling my daughters the same thing. Why are Negro people in general so envious of one another? I will never know. My mother told me she had an opportunity to work in city hall for a famous judge. She mentioned it to a "so-called friend." For some reason, my mother did not get that job! A pastor once said, "Sometimes, you don't need to tell everybody what God has placed on your heart. Keep your mouth shut!"

When I was sixteen, Nana was not getting around as well as she used too. So cleaning and cooking for her was a pleasure. The only chore I hated was ironing sheets. Back in the day, spray starch or steam irons had not been invented. Nana would take a bottle and make small holes in the top and fill the bottle up with water. We had to shake the water from the bottle onto the sheet. Next, we placed the iron on the wet area to make the stream, thus getting rid of the majority of wrinkles. After suppertime was the best time because Nana would tell me stories about the South and poor white people who lived down the road from her house.

John F Kennedy's Assassination

During my tenth grade English class, we were interrupted through the Public Address System, with a notification President John F. Kennedy had been assassinated. All my teachers were crying, and school was dismissed early. I could not believe what I was hearing. I quickly ran home and turned on the television. A TV news station showed First Lady Jacqueline Kennedy in a suit that looked like it had blood on it. We still did not have a color television yet, so in black and white you could not tell what color someone was wearing. I remember seeing Vice President Lyndon B. Johnson being sworn in as the President of the United States on Air Force One, the name of the president's plane. There was a strange quietness over my small town. No cars were moving. I had to look outside to see if anyone was moving. No one was outside. When my mother arrived home, I could tell she had been crying.

Assassination of John F. Kennedy

President Kennedy with his wife, Jacqueline, and Governor of Texas John Connally in the presidential limousine, minutes before the president's assassination.

Location Dealey Plaza
Dallas, Texas

Coordinates 32.77903°N 96.80867°W

Date November 22, 1963
12:30 p.m. (Central Time)

Target	John F. Kennedy
Attack type	Sniper style assassination
Weapon(s)	6.5 × 52 mm Italian Carcano M91/38 bolt-action rifle
Deaths	1 killed (President Kennedy)
Injured (non-fatal)	2 wounded (Governor Connally and James Tague)
Perpetrator	Lee Harvey Oswald

This is the picture of where the shots came from that killed President Kennedy.

Chapter 19
Being Nobody's Daughter has a Negative Effect

In my senior year in high school, I ran for Homecoming Queen. The committee had eliminated the girls down to five; I was one of those five girls. All we needed to win was to sell the most tickets and memorize the acceptance speech, a piece a cake! At that time, my mother worked three jobs, one at a cleaners, a restaurant, and a third, as a dispatcher for a taxi company. My mother met many people, and she helped me sell many tickets. Somehow, I figured out how much each girl had sold, right before the deadline, and I knew I needed about one hundred dollars more to win. Therefore, I quickly called my "biological" dad. I pleaded with him to bring me the money before 3:30pm on a Thursday. That was the deadline for all monies to be in. He promised me he would meet me by the girl's gym by 3:00pm. If that Negro showed up, then cows fly. I ended up coming in third place.

Throughout my life, I waited and prayed for that man to step up and be a man and be a real father. He never did. It was my mother who continued to make me be respectful to him and his new family. Additionally, he lied to me so many times saying he was coming to pick me up and take me places. He never once came through on any promises he made to me. However, I always waited and prayed that he would until my stepfather, who I consider my real dad, came along and took the place of him in my soul.

I learned early just because you can make a baby does not mean you are a father. I cared less because my heart had hardened so much for liars. Unfortunately, that man's behavior affected my life for a long time. I subconsciously blamed every negative feeling, circumstance, emotion, and just being out of control on my biological father. It was his lack of knowledge concerning being a real man that I blamed the most.

Dr. Stacey Nickleberry

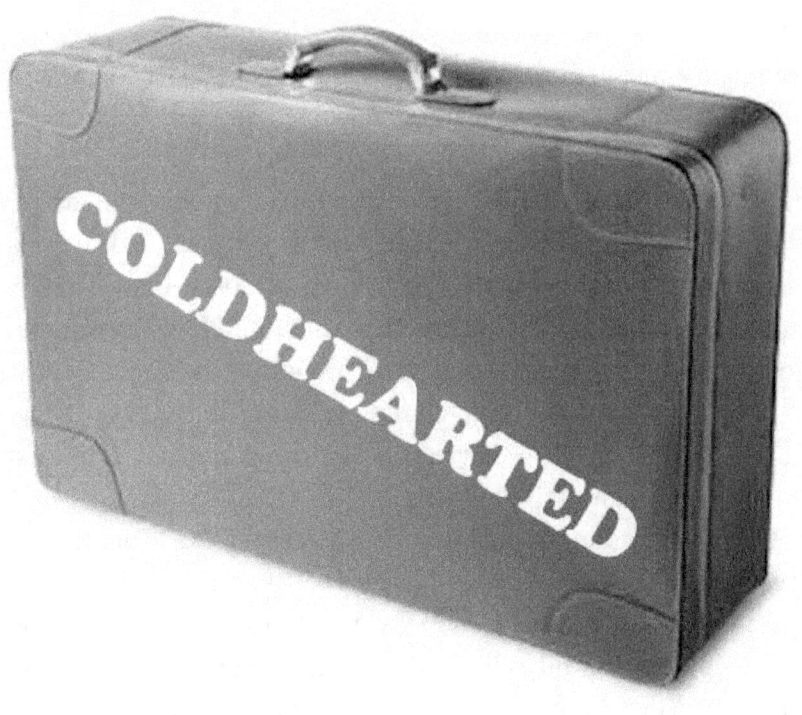

Chapter 20
Teenage Social Life

I watched American Bandstand as a teenager.
Gladys Knight and the Pips were my favorite guests.

The only music television program when I was growing up was American Bandstand. I would watch that program every time it came on. My best girlfriend lived across the hall from me, and we had a lot in common. American Bandstand inspired my friends to start a singing group, patterning ourselves after Diana Ross and the Supremes. We really thought Motown Records would discover our singing group. By that time, we had really started to like boys at the same time, around eighth or ninth grade. Her boyfriend was named Ronald. He did not look very cute to me because my girlfriend looked a lot better. I never had just one boyfriend; I had several. Although certain boys would say I was their girlfriend, I would never say they were my boyfriends.

My best friend, Pat went to a different church, and the pastor would pick her up every Friday night for youth choir practice. We were what some adults would call "fast." However, my best girlfriend was "faster" than I was! She told me about a blue light dance that was happening on Friday night. She wanted to go, but her mother and my mother did not believe in girls dating before sixteen. She said for me to ask my mother if I could go to choir practice with her. She had already called the church and told the pastor she could not come one particular Friday to choir practice. She called a taxi for an address a couple of doors down from our house, and when the taxi driver blew his horn, she pretended it was the pastor's horn blowing. Then, my girlfriend knocked on my door and said, "The pastor is here." It worked like a charm. My mother did not look out the window to check to see if it really was the pastor's car. We laughed all the way down the street because her plan had worked.

Let me tell you about that dance. First, it was in the middle of winter, about twenty degrees outside. The dance was at least twelve blocks from our house, and in a garage with a blue light. It cost twenty-five cents to get in. It was crowded and stinky. Her boyfriend was there, and the other guys were as ugly as he was. There was no way I was going to dance any slow dances with the likes of them. It seemed that every song they played was a slow song. So, I found a space on the wall and stood. There I stayed. Several people tried to make me dance, but I was no fool. I saw what they were doing to the other girls. I knew if I danced with one of those guys, and he tried that with me, it was going to be a fight! We left the blue light dance in time to get home about the time the pastor usually dropped my girlfriend off after choir practice. That was my first blue light dance and my last.

A little later, out of nowhere, my mother packed and announced we were moving. I was glad when we moved into a predominately-white neighborhood, so I would not have to tell my best girlfriend that my mother had found out about the blue light dance. We did meet up again, years later. She is very successful and owns her own business, and guess what? She also moved to California.

Growing up in Gary, Indiana was a blast. There were so many things to do as a teenager. There were two movie theaters in Downtown Gary, a roller-skating rink, near Nana's house, a football field and basketball stadium. I do not ever remember being scared to go out at night. I would even walk through a park to get to my house at night.

Many basketball games were played here.
I especially loved those against Roosevelt and Froebel High School.

The Assassination of Dr. Martin Luther King, Jr.

Dr. King was an American clergyman, activist, and prominent leader of the African American civil rights movement and Nobel Peace Prize laureate who became known for his advancement of civil rights by using civil disobedience. He was assassinated at the Lorraine Motel in Memphis, Tennessee on April 4, 1968, at the age of 39. King was rushed to St. Joseph's Hospital, where he was pronounced dead at 7:05PM that evening. James Earl Ray, a fugitive from the Missouri State Penitentiary, was arrested in London at Heathrow Airport, extradited to the United States, and charged with the crime. On March 10, 1969, Ray entered a plea of guilty and was sentenced to 99 years in the Tennessee State Penitentiary. Ray later made many attempts to withdraw his guilty plea and be tried by a jury but was unsuccessful; he died in prison on April 23, 1998, at the age of 70.

The King family and others believe that the assassination was carried out by a conspiracy involving the U.S. government, as alleged by Loyd Jowers in 1993, and that James Earl Ray was a scapegoat. In a 1999 civil trial that did not name the U.S. government as a defendant and sought $100 from Jowers, the jury ruled Loyd Jowers and others, including unspecified governmental agencies, were all part of the conspiracy to kill Martin Luther King, Jr.

How the Citizens Reacted After Dr. King's Assassination

In 1968, I was working at a major company, on the 3-11pm shift. When we heard that Dr. Martin Luther King had been assassinated, there were about eleven African Americans working there compared to six hundred whites. We could tell by their faces, the white people were glad and at the same time scared. They announced that the plant was closing and for everybody to go home.The company paid us for the rest of the day. As we walked to our cars, there was a strange glow in the sky (towards Chicago).

As I drove home, I saw gangs of people walking towards downtown. When I got home, my mother said, "People are rioting. You are to stay inside the house." She also said, "Blacks had tried to get to the Loop in Chicago, but the police had cornered that plot off." Black people ended up burning down their own neighborhoods out of frustration, I suppose. I just knew in my heart that J. Edgar Hoover, the head of the FBI had something to do with King's assassination.

During the riots after Martin Luther King Jr.'s killing, 350 people were arrested for looting and published accounts say nine to eleven people died. Chicago police, shown here with rifles at the ready, crouch behind a patrol car to take cover from a sniper.
(Tribune photo by Don C.)

Dr. Stacey Nickleberry

Chapter 21
Pre-College Days: Partying until I Dropped

After high school, my mother pulled some strings, and with one word, I received the best job in my life up to that point. The Anderson was a windshield factory in Gary, Indiana. The pay was very good. I was able to move into my own apartment, and my biological dad co-signed for my new car. He later lied and told everyone he bought me a car. Really, what a liar! After nineteen years, he was finally trying to do something for me. Give me a break! I was able to stand on my own, thanks to my mom who had taught me well. I thank God. I was raised by a strong black woman. After watching my mom work three jobs and make sure her children received a good education, I applaud her for a job well done.

I was nineteen years old and engaged to my high school sweetheart. We had both attended Froebel High School. He played football and was the captain of the team. He was one handsome dude. While I worked to save more money to attend college, he was already in college.

While my fiancé was in college, I figured I might as well get my party time out of the way. My hometown of Gary is only thirty miles from Chicago, Illinois. In the early 70's, Chicago was one of my spots for clubbing. One of my favorite places was *Guys and Dolls* and the *Burning Spear*. We would party from sun down to sunrise.

One night, my girls and I went to the *Burning Spear*. We were dancing to the song, "The Roof is on Fire!" All of a sudden, someone yelled, "The roof is on fire!" I thought that was all part of the act, until I looked up and saw that the roof was really on fire. I have had so many narrow escapes like that when I could have lost my life. But, God covered me, and unknown to me, He had a plan.

Us working women seldom had money to travel to Chicago to party. On those occasions when we did not have gas money, the next hot spot was *Sonny Peterson*, a club in East Chicago. To help you understand how crazy young folk were, many partygoers in Gary would go to *Sonny Peterson*. The club was located in a basement. To get to the basement, there were at least thirty stairs we had to go down. There was one way in and one way out. On a good Saturday night, at least one hundred people would be crowded on the dance floor and drinking at *Sonny Peterson*. Many people could have died if a fire or fight had occurred because there is no way everybody could get up those stairs without falling and stepping over someone. (God does watch over babies and fools.)

During the 1970's, my time of clubbing, I recall meeting Michael Jackson and his brothers while they were performing in a place called the *Gary Armory* on Highway 20. At the time, Michael was around five years old. *The Jackson Five* were not well-known, yet. However, I knew then those young men were going to make it big!

After his graduation from college, my fiancé and I were married. He got a teaching job, and it was my turn to attend college. I entered Indiana University three years after my high school classmates, because I wanted to have a car and be able to pay my own tuition. To earn money, my job, assembling windshield wipers at the Anderson Company, allowed me to buy my first car within two years of employment. I had a new car and savings in the bank, so I was off to college to Indiana University. I also worked at Methodist Hospital a few hours as a part-time laboratory receptionist where my biological father was a nurse.

My mother never gave up trying to get that deadbeat man to step up and be a father and wanted me to try to develop a relationship with him because she had lost her father at the age of nine. I loved my mother and never wanted to disappoint her, so I went along with the program. However, I was able to see he was never up to any good, and I really wished he never existed. (God, forgive me, because as much as I felt abandoned by my father, I still needed him.)

Getting back to my hospital job, my biological father arranged for me to work in the laboratory as a receptionist. On the third day on the job, a nurse brought in a container with the remains of a fetus. I took one look at it, and I was out for the count. I fainted. That incident convinced me that nursing was absolutely not for me, and a career in teaching was becoming more intriguing.

When I was nineteen, my biological father failed to understand I did not want anything from him because when I needed him, he was too busy or never kept his promises. But, really it was my turn to show him just how nasty I could be for all I felt he had not done to me. Karma is a mug!

All of a sudden, he wanted to be a father. It was a little too late. He had established another family, and from that family I had a baby sister, who was ten years younger. One thing, I believed yet have no proof was he was a better father to my sister than he ever was to me. I loved my baby sister, so I tried to do more for her than what was ever done for me by our father. I would buy her clothes, toys, etc. I never received anything from my "so-called biological father," except forty dollars a month for child support. I was surprised he paid so little. You would have thought it was a fortune from the way he abandoned me. Finding out he had not paid enough money to make up for his behavior made him even more deplorable. My entire childhood was filled with painful memories of me waiting for him to come by and spend time with me. Because the pain was so great and consuming, my behavior towards men was unbelievable. Any little thing that made me reflect back to the feeling of abandonment would take my anger to the edge. I would get so angry. I believe I could have killed somebody. But, God protected me through all of that.

Dr. Stacey Nickleberry

Chapter 22
Our First African American Mayor

As I was working various jobs, my mother went into politics. She worked in Gary City Hall with Mayor Richard Hatcher. Voters elected Gary's first African American mayor, Richard G. Hatcher, in 1967. He was elected to four four-year consecutive terms. My mother was also the first female to become Precinct Committee Person in our predominately white neighborhood and was instrumental in assisting Mayor Hatcher's election as mayor of Gary.

Mr. Anderson
(Owner of the first windshield factory in Gary, Indiana)

Mr. Anderson founded The Anderson Company (ANCO), a manufacturer of automobile accessories, in South Bend, Ind., in 1918. In 1923, he relocated to Gary, Ind., where ANCO employed a significant number of people in the production of refillable windshield wiper blades, Anderson's signature invention. During World War II, Anderson co-founded the Automotive Council for War Production in Detroit. He received the Freedom Foundation Award in 1950 and the Jefferson Medal of the New Jersey Patent Law Association in 1954. He was posthumously inducted into the Automotive Hall of Fame in 1972. This was an important milestone in my life. It was a very difficult time in American History for African American employment opportunities, as more were available than in the past. White people were forced to work amongst us and vice-versa. Working side-by-side with white people really gave me insight to what the corporate world was about and how to succeed. With what I learned, I knew getting my behind in a college was a wise choice. Taking orders was not how I saw my life. Giving orders was more my forte.

Changing Demographics Led to African Americans being the Majority Ethnic Group in Gary, Indiana

Richard Hatcher
(Former Mayor of Gary, Indiana)

Beginning in the 1960s, Gary's population decreased through "white flight" to the suburbs. By 1990, the population was made up of 80 percent African Americans. Hatcher's administration improved housing conditions in the city and helped obtain federal job training programs. In 1982, the Genesis Convention Center was built in the heart of Gary's downtown to help in the revitalization of the business district.

Gary made great progress during the 1960s and 1970s in reducing its air pollution caused by smoke from factories and steel mills. The amount of impurities in the air dropped nearly 60 percent from 1966 to 1976. The city issued nearly $180 million in revenue bonds to help U.S. Steel reduce its pollution at local facilities.

The loss of population in Gary during the 1980s, almost 25 percent, was larger than that of any other U.S. city. By 1995, the city's population was 85 percent African American. That year, Scott L. King, who is white, confounded observers when he won an upset victory in the mayoral election. Apparently, King's energy and vision for Gary has transcended racial bounds, as he is still at its helm as the city reaches its Centennial.

Still battling poverty, unemployment, a shrinking population, and a less-than-stellar reputation, in the dawn of the twenty-first century, the focus of community leaders and businesses in Gary has been to revitalize Gary's downtown and make the city attractive to visitors.

Dr. Stacey Nickleberry

Chapter 23
College Days:
Indiana University

Naturally, I was the only African American female on campus with a brand new blue two-door Barracuda. It was not long before the car brought attention, and I was quickly noticed by sororities. I pledged Alpha Kappa Alpha my second year. The AKA girls were the popular girls and very stuck up! You had to act and dress a certain way to belong. The opposite sorority on campus was Delta Sigma Theta; they were a mess! In other words, they were the campus tramps!

When my mother found out that I had pledged AKA, she hit the roof. After all, she was a Delta. All my relatives in the South were Deltas. Life as an AKA during family reunions was not very pleasant for me. However, everyone in my family knew I was a fighter. I did not care how big or small a person may have been in stature. Win, loose, or draw, I was never afraid to fight. I could not take anyone pushing the wrong button, or all hell was going to break loose. Finally, after many years, several younger cousins also broke tradition and pledged AKA. Thank you cousins for keeping it real! Looking back on that period of my life, it really was not that serious, and sororities have no reason to be against one another because we are all in the same struggle.

History: My Major in College

I had already settled on the fact my major would be United States History. I wanted to know what made this country so racist. Nana had told me so many stories about Africa and slavery, but I could not figure out why white people wanted us to go back to Africa during the Marcus Garvey Movement.

As I began my major in United States History as a sophomore at the University of Indiana, I remember being so excited that I would finally learn why the United States was so racist. Once I enrolled in my first history class, my professor finally brought up the topic "Slavery in America." He said, "Slaves were very happy to be owned by white people because they were well taken care of and did not have a care in this world." I had waited a long time and that professor made the most racist statement I had ever heard. I do not remember how the words came out of my mouth, in a predominantly white university in a predominantly white class, but I remember raising my hand and asking the question, "Why would anyone think slaves were happy being forced to come to a place they knew nothing about, with a people that hated them and treated them cruelly?"

I could not believe I had waited all that time to hear the truth about racism in America and ended up with a racist professor. That professor turned about three shades of red when I corrected him.

He totally ignored my comments and went right on talking about how Africans were barbaric and needed to be trained. I politely excused myself from that class, and I immediately dropped the course.

I was amazed to find such a small number of African American students on Indiana University's campus and the fact we did not stick together. Then, I remember what Nana had taught me. Nana said the envy and jealousy between Africans/African Americans started back in Africa. You may be shocked; I was too, when I first heard this. In Africa, not all Africans liked each other; there were as many varieties of Africans as there are many variations of African Americans today. There were all shapes, colors and sizes all over Africa and different African languages and customs, depending on the area and tribe. This may be a factor that needed addressing because we as a people have been bamboozled, meaning we have no idea that we were kings and queens in Africa. Our culture, language, and religion have been stolen and destroyed. To get back to where we were before the Mayflower, we will have to read and research and stop fighting one another.

During the late sixties and early seventies, my hair was like Angela Davis'. I had a huge afro, as did most of my ethnic background on campus. Conversations began with a few black students discussing conditions on the Indiana University Campus. It was not long before I joined the Black Panther Movement on campus. We were going to change the world.

We staged sit-ins on the doorsteps of the president of the university. We demanded additional African American History classes be included in the curriculum and that the university hire more African American professors to teach courses. I really do not believe it was our little group of twenty African American students that brought about the changes on the campus of Indiana

University, but the totality of all the Freedom Marches throughout the United States. It was time for a change in America.

Shortly after that, my little radical group decided to join the freedom marches in the South. So one Friday night, six of us jumped into a car headed down Interstate 95 towards the state of Mississippi. Somewhere, we made a wrong turn and ended up on a dirt road. It was very dark, and we could not see any lights for miles around. Suddenly, a police car drove up behind us. (I believe police in Mississippi back then had secret hideouts in the cornfields.) We never saw where the police car came from.

All of a sudden, we saw a light shining into the back of our car. We stopped, of course. The officers walked over to the car, placing a flashlight into the car, and asked where we were headed. The driver of our car quickly lied and said he was looking for his aunt's house, in Duran, Mississippi. The officers were not buying that. One of the officers with a flashlight said, in a rough voice, "Your license tags say you all are from Indiana. We don't need any Northerners down here stirring up our niggers. So, if I were you, I would back this car up and headback up the Interstate 95 until you see Indiana. And if I see this car again, and you niggers, they'll never find your bodies!" I cannot remember how we got out of that area. The next thing I knew, we were headed towards home. As I look back on that situation, I believe God has a place in time for everybody. He knows who He wants for His purpose, and during that time in history, the Civil Rights sit-in was definitely not my assignment. That was the end of my militant era.

Dr. Stacey Nickleberry

Chapter 24
Married too Young

When I married my high school sweetheart, we had a beautiful wedding. While planning for the wedding, I thought I would do the right thing and give my so-called "biological" father the privilege of walking me down the aisle. My main reason for making that decision was my mother expressing it was the proper thing to do. I wanted the only dad that treated me like a daughter to have that privilege. However, my dad told me to let my biological dad walk me down the aisle.

During the reception, we noticed a whole case of liquor had strangely disappeared as well my biological father. It was during that time in my life that I realized how mentally messed up he really was. Maybe some of those traits had been handed down to me. For a long time, his family thought he had paid for my lavish wedding, which included twelve bridesmaids and bridegrooms. I was blessed to have my newlywed husband's family assist us with paying for the wedding and no one else, for the record.

For those of you on my biological father's side of the family, including his sister and brothers, probably out of plain ignorance, I have forgiven you for your rejection. In the long run, you did me a favor. It made me more determined to succeed. I turned all that anger over to the Lord a long time ago. I hold no bitterness towards anyone, past, present or future. But, let me say this, I am not perfect and do not pretend to be. I am very outspoken and will let you know just what I think. However, I am older and have let go of a lot of the anger. I realize it serves no purpose in my life. I want to present the best examples for my own children, grandchildren, and myself.

My new husband and I moved into a two-bedroom Cape-Cod style house in the Horseman area of Gary a predominantly white neighborhood in the late 1960's. The home was purchased by my husband's parents. We were blessed tremendously. There were few young couples who can say they moved into a house of their own in the late 1960's. My husband taught middle school students, while I began courses at Indiana University.

Although we were blessed, we had our ups and downs just as other married couples. I remember one day, I had become angry with my husband and starting throwing dishes down the basement stairs. He was standing in the doorway of the kitchen. When I finally settled down, he said, "Now, I guess you're going to have to clean that mess up." He turned and walked away. I realized breaking things would not get me what I wanted, so I came up with other tactics. (We still laugh about that day.)

Unfortunately, the marriage lasted less than a year. It was no fault of his; I take total blame for the marriage going south. The divorce was due to my immaturity, not understanding the seriousness of the marriage vows, my selfishness, and a lot of anger. Additionally, I carried a lot of baggage that had not been resolved. The annulment cost less than the wedding. Looking back on that situation, I now realize I was too young to be anyone's wife. I had so much baggage that I had not taken the time to analyze. I believe that I masked the hurt I was feeling from anyone that loved me.

Nobody's Daughter

What I regret most about that marriage were leaving my in-laws. My in-laws were the best people in this world. I truly loved them dearly and disappointing them hurt me the most. Additionally, I felt horrible disappointing him and his family. When issues are unresolved, one person can really mess up another person's life. And it may be a person who did not deserve having to deal with the messed-up baggage.

My ex-mother-in-law Ms. Clara was like a mother to me. We talked about everything. I credit her for the good cook I have become today. Ms. C and I had a lot in common. Although Ms. C was petite, she carried a big stick. She would not back down from a good fight. Her husband Hank, my ex-father-in-law, was great too and the best father-in-law. He would make fabulous tamales and BBQ. I wished I had received those recipes; they would most definitely be a moneymaker today.

Ms. C and Hank Sr. were from Mississippi and moved to Gary, Indiana because of the Steel Mills. Also, Hank Sr. was born with a veil over his face, and like Nana, he could see ghosts. Hank Sr. would tell scary ghost stories. He did not call ghosts "GHOSTS." He called them "Hanks." And he did not call the werewolf "WEREWOLF," but "Werry-wolf." He was truly a stand-up comedian before Moms Mobley and Red Fox came on the scene.

Every Sunday, Ms. C, Hank, and I would go to the Chicago state line to get the liquor supply for the week while Hank Jr. was playing football at college. Hank Sr. loved to drink, especially after working all day in the US Steel Mill. He enjoyed drinking his liquor while lying on the living room floor, until he was sloppy drunk. Ms. C would get so angry with him. That is usually how arguments between them would occur. Hank Sr. never really minded Ms. C fussing with him. He always laughed at everything she said. I imagined that is why they were married over forty years. Together, they could have been a stand-up comedian act.

One night when Hank Jr. was home from college, his family had a party. Hank Sr. had become so drunk he began pulling his pants down in front of company. Ms. C hit him so hard; he sobered up very quickly. Those were the most humorous and happiest times of my life. There was never a dull moment. I would laugh until tears came into my eyes.

On another occasion, I remember Hank Sr. found a dog and brought it home. I called him "Soona," meaning 'soon to be anything'! Hank Sr. liked to feed everybody and anybody. If you came to their house, you had to eat. Hank Sr. treated the dog no differently. He fed that dog table food.

On one particular Sunday, Hank Sr. decided to take the dog with us to the Chicago state line. Right after we passed through East Chicago, the dog got sick and threw up all over the back seat of the car. That was a stinky mess and the longest drive to the State line and the most unpleasant. Ms. C fussed about that dog all the way there and all the way back.

During the times we spent together, Ms. C. had a lot of stories she told me about her life in the South. She said, in her hometown, white people were poorer than the average Negro. She said her mother would receive the Sears catalog in the mail ever so often, and when she finished with the catalog, she would give it to the white woman down the road. Now, the white woman was very friendly with Ms. C's parents, because her family had a garden and raised chickens. During the Depression, her parents fed many poor white people, including the white woman that used the Sear's catalog pages to wallpaper her home.

Chapter 25
Not Having Nana was Too Much for Me to Bear

During my second year in college in 1970's, Nana went to the hospital. She had eaten some spoiled food from the refrigerator that poisoned her stomach. I felt so bad, because I had not been there to cook for her. When I went into her hospital room, Grandma Lee was there, and I just knew Nana was never coming home. I stayed with her for several weeks, trying to make her feel better. We laughed about the time I came over to visit her wearing a mini-skirt. She told me to go back home and put on some clothes.

After my visit to the hospital, I knew Nana wanted to go home and be with the Lord. She would often tell me that when she could no longer get around, she would rather go and be with the Lord. Grandma Lee had retired from the Railroad in Chicago and had moved in with Nana. Grandma Lee also had married a very nice man named James.

Nana stayed in the hospital for three weeks. One night, while sleeping, I was suddenly awakened by the scent of Nana around 12:00 midnight. I will never forget that. At that moment, my phone rang, and my mother told me Nana had passed away. I asked her at what time, and she said, "Around midnight." Now, I know that some religious people say what I experienced is not possible. They would say that was an evil spirit, but I disagree. I know that was Nana saying goodbye to me because we were just that close. I know in my heart that Nana would not leave this earth without saying goodbye to me. Therefore, I just believe when I see Nana again, in heaven, and I will let her tell me herself!

Nana's funeral was small and personable. A few of her friends, who could still get around, attended. Among those in attendance were church members and the immediate family. I was holding up pretty well during the funeral, until the choir began to sing Nana's favorite song: "Precious Lord!" At that moment, I could not stop crying. It was not a quiet cry, but loud! Grandma Lee looked at me as if she wanted to slap the hell out of me. Luckily, for me we were in a church. (My family strongly believed you moan at home).

The next day, Grandma Lee asked me to come over and help pack Nana's things. As we were going through her clothes, we learned Nana had money stashed everywhere. We found hundreds of dollars in dresses, coats, and apron pockets. By the time we had everything packed, we counted five thousand dollars. When I thought about it, I recalled I had never seen Nana go to a bank. I knew she collected money from her renters and received money from playing the numbers. It suddenly dawned on me at that moment: Nana did not trust the bank. After all, Nana lived through the Great Depression (1930's) when the banks folded and millions of people lost their money. Nana had her own banking system. I also believe Nana had money hidden in other places. Nevertheless, I guess that is another question I need to ask Nana when I see her again in heaven.

Grandma Lee lived in the house owned by my Nana on 24th and Adams, in Gary, Indiana, until my mother moved to California into her grandfather's house. Sometime after my mother moved to California, she sent for Grandma Lee. Grandma Lee's husband had passed away, and my mother made sure her mother would not be left alone. The house on 24th and Adams has probably been torn down, and I bet there is money somewhere on that property.

Grandma Lee found Nana's "Lone Ranger Gun." I asked her what she was going to do with it, and she said, "I'm going to keep it!" I thought to myself, *I hope no one makes my Grandma Lee angry, especially if she is carrying that gun.* You may think Tyler Perry's character Madea is crazy, but Madea has nothing on Grandma Lee.

Nobody's Daughter

Just to give you an example of Grandma Lee's temperament. One Thanksgiving before Nana's passing, my mother called everyone to the table to eat. Nana wanted to carry her purse to the table with her, and Grandma Lee said, "Put that purse down. You don't need to carry that purse to the table." I had grown older and braver, and I said to Grandma Lee, "She can carry her purse to the table if she wants." Grandma Lee grabbed me by my throat with both her hands; I thought she would choke me to death. It took my mother, Nana, my sister and my brother to pull her off me. I could not eat or swallow without pain for weeks.

As time passed, everyone my age was getting married and having babies. During my junior year at the university, I married my second husband. We had met when I was twelve, and he was thirteen. His uncle was a preacher (the one that used to pick up my girlfriend, Pat and I for choir practice on Fridays), and I sang in the choir with my best girlfriend who could really sing. During that time, I was still carrying baggage.

My husband's name was Jim. From that marriage, I had two children: Tyese and Turron. Life seemed to go fine for a while. The marriage failed because of lack of ambition on his part and my messed up attitude on the other. In addition, he would probably say, he could never do anything good enough for me, which may be the truth. The reality is, I did not know what good was. Everything had to be my way or no way. In my opinion, if you just did what I said, we would not have any problems.

Neither of us had a clue about what a spiritual marriage or commitment was about. Although we went to church every Sunday and heard the Gospel preached, we had no personal relationship with God. In fact, it was our belief that if you behaved as a good person, you were going to heaven. It was our opinion, at least I believed, only murderers and the like were going to hell. Even Jim's uncle, the preacher, during the early years of our growing up had no revelation of the gospel, either. I do not know if he was called by God or just went into ministry on his own.

My husband's aunt Lillie was a sweetheart. She had the presence of Jesus. I never heard her say a negative word about anyone, and she treated everyone well. In addition, Jim's sister Margie was another Madea. She is still crazy acting to this day. She and I got along well. I guess because we were both crazy acting. During the 1970's, we did not fight. Instead, we could tear you up with our mouths, without laying a hand on you. Jim and his sister Marg were over six feet tall. He was very good at sports and played for a semi-pro team before we married. I believed he regretted not having the opportunity to go professional.

Long after Jim and I divorced, I realized I was still looking for my father's presence. I was angry with him. Therefore, until I addressed my issues, no one would be able to fulfill my needs. I really regret separating the children from their father at an early age. Tyese took the divorce the hardest. She loved her dad and to this day, they have a very strong bond. Turron was only two years old; therefore, he did not have the opportunity to form a bond with his dad. I believe because of that he does not have a close relationship with his dad today.

One day, my mother called me over to her house and told my sister, brother and me, she was moving to Los Angeles, California. Great-Grandma Debra had passed away and my mother's grandfather needed her to take care of him. I could not believe how calmly my mother explained leaving me. I thought maybe she was leaving in a couple of months, but she informed us she would be leaving at the end of the week. I could not imagine my mother leaving a pink Cadillac and a man who loved her dearly in the matter of a week. Although we were adults, I realized I needed her the most.

Despite my immediate feeling of loss and abandonment, I told her I was happy for her. My great-grandfather had accumulated wealth, owned his own home, and invested well and could retire her. Who would not take that offer? Once again, I felt rejected and abandoned. Even though I was in my early thirties, I felt I still needed my mother.

After the divorce, I moved into my mother's house. My brother moved in too. It was a nice arrangement. I started a traveling club at my school and set it up where I would take as many students as possible during the summer to California to all the amusement parks and other attractions in and out of the California region.

In the beginning of the school year, with my principal's permission, I sent out a flyer outlining the itinerary for the trip to California in June, the cost and travel expense. Immediately after school was out, we were off to California on Amtrak. During that particular summer, I took eighty students and four adult chaperons to Los Angeles, California, including my seven-year-old daughter. The children were well behaved.

However, before we could pull off from Chicago, the conductor asked who was in charge of all the loud children. When I approached him to inquire about any problems, he said, "Only ten children at a time can go to the snack bar." I said, "Excuse you. It will take all day before all eighty children can get a snack, and I am not having it!" He said, "I really don't care what you're having. That's the rule on my train." I said, "I hope your name is Mr. Amtrak, because you are going to have it!" (He had the nerve to dictate what a tour group of children can do on a train that does not belong to him).

He said, "Madam, all eighty children can be served, but there are other passengers on this train that might want a snack. You really need to be considerate of other people's needs also." I could not believe that man put me in my place. I had never had a man talk to me in a strong demanding way without being rude or disrespectful. He just spoke matter-of-factly, and that was it.

Then, he said, "Let me buy you a cup of coffee. I can see you are already having a rough day." That man later became my third husband (Mr. Nickleberry).

When the children and I arrived to California, my mother met us at the hotel in Hollywood where all eighty plus of us were staying for five days and four nights. The conductor and I had exchanged phone numbers, and he called after all the children had gone to bed. Although my soon-to-be husband did not sing, he had a light complexion and hazel eyes that reminded me of Smokey Robinson. When he spoke, it was gentle yet firm. After a year of dating long-distance, he finally asked me to marry him; then, he moved my two children and me to California. I was so excited to be near my mother. My mother and I would talk three to five times a day on the phone. Even after I visited her, we still called one another and talked more. My mom was like a sister to me, after I became an adult.

My new husband and I got along fine. We never fought or argued about anything. Every time he saw that hurricane rise up in me, he would gently settle me down, quickly! Usually, I would get impatient about something or something was not happening fast enough for me. He would always say, "Take a deep breath. Getting yourself upset is not going to make it happen any faster. In addition, hollering and screaming is going to give you a stroke." I never could get a negative reaction out of him.

One time, I washed his eighty-dollar silk shirt. He said, "Before you wash, read the labels." I thought for sure he would be angry. He loved to dress; he probably had at least a hundred suits and shoes to match. He was very neat and particular. One thing I forgot to add: he was thirteen years older than I was. He had served in the Korean War and had two adult daughters.

In other words, he had been there and done that! At the time, he was just what I needed in my life to calm me down! His daughters' mother had done a wonderful job raising very respectable young women. LV and Jacque both had young daughters when their dad and I married. My new husband told me how the divorce of their mother had hurt him tremendously. He wanted to be a good father and grandfather. I believe I gave him that opportunity.

At the time, my sister and brother were still in Gary and my mother would cry often, because she wanted all of us together. My great-grandfather would assure her that all her children would eventually move to California, including Grandma Lee who was still married at the time and living in Nana's house. My great-grandfather was one of the founders of the First African Methodist Episcopal Church in California (F.A.M.E.) He was a member when the church was first located on Townes Street in Los Angeles. My mother soon joined the church, after arriving in California. Once her entire family arrived in California, we all attended her church. I raised all my children in F.A.M.E. under Pastor Cecil Murray.

It was not long before I became pregnant with twins. During delivery, my husband swore he would be right by my side, until he saw the head of one of the babies. At that moment, he totally disappeared. Melva and Melvin, Jr. were born, six pounds five ounces and six pounds four ounces, respectively. My husband was one proud papa. Everybody marveled at how beautiful the babies were, especially Melva. My philosophy was not to spoil Melva because she would get the attention anyway, but to carry Melvin, Jr. all the time.

Tyese was seven when the twins were born and a great little helper to me. She would hold Melva and feed her a bottle while I had Melvin, Jr. My husband still worked for Amtrak and was out thirteen days and in ten. Therefore, it was hard with four little children while he was gone. Turron was only three and still under me all the time.

My husband's sister Jean loved those twins. Whenever she had time off from the hospital, where she was a nurse, she came and took the twins for a while. Therefore, I could get some things done around the house. I loved her dearly. In fact, she pierced Melva's ears when she was three months old herself. Jean never saw the twins reach their fifth birthday, as she died of throat cancer.

My twin's godmother, Margie was my first best friend, whom I met when I moved to California. Her husband Acie was my husband's best friend. She also assisted me with the twins. Twins are no joke! The first few days after bringing them home from the hospital, I did not sleep a wink. I would get one to sleep; then, the other one would wake up. Finally, my husband called the doctor and jokingly told him I was sending one of the twins back, because I was not getting any sleep! The doctor immediately understood the dilemma and told my husband not to let the twins set their own hours. When one twin woke up, I was to wake the other and feed them at the same time, so they would sleep at the same time. What wisdom! I also realized that I kept getting their bottles mixed up. One baby was on Enfamil and the other on Similac, so I had to label the bottles. I learned so many little things through trial and error. At least, I knew to give babies water, which was something I did not know when Tyese was born. If it had not been for my mother noticing the milk caked on her tongue, I would have never learned. When she saw the milk, her immediate reaction was to boil water, cool it down, and give to my first-born her first taste of water. I thought everything the baby needed was in the formula. Strangely, today that is what the new mothers are told: everything is in the formula.

My husband's mother, Charlie was a very private person and greatly misunderstood by most. She and I got along fine. She suffered a lot of pain from being misunderstood. My husband's younger brother had committed suicide at sixteen, and I never heard their family discuss the reason. My husband never wanted to talk about it, either. His mother liked to play the horses, and so did my mother. My mother was good at numbers and had come up with a system to figure out the winner, by adding the postposition of the horse, his/her weigh and the jockey's name. The first place winner total must add up to ten, and the second place horse must add up to a nine. Now, ten and nine can be made in several different combinations, such as fifty-five is a ten, forty-five is a nine, and so on. I was not a mathematician, but I could figure out the winners the majority of the time, but I was not good with figuring out the nines or second place winners. Remember, Coach Dennis, my math teacher.

Every Wednesday-Sunday, I had a winning horse. If I were smart, I would be wealthy now. When my new mother-in-law realized I had this gift, our friendship really took off. I remember telling her that my mother and I were going to the Hollywood Park racetrack and were going to play a horse in the first race called Ms. Cockatoo. The horse with her name and jockey combined numbers were a ten. She said, "That horse hasn't been out since last year. No way she will win." She based her horse winners on the formula of the Race Forum. I said, "That's the horse I'm playing." The horse won, paying eighty dollars to win. From then on, she called to ask me what horse I had selected for all the races.

My husband's mother and father were from Texas. His father had passed away before I came to California. I remember my mother-in-law telling me he formed the first Black Pullmans Union for Amtrak in California. He later retired and began a Bail Bonds Office on Central Street located in the Florence Area of Los Angeles. I know she had a brother and his son had twins. Going back to a precious observation, she was very private, and I never asked questions. As the twins grew, they loved to visit both grandmothers; everyone spoiled them, especially their older sisters.

Times were tough for me after leaving a good teaching position in Gary and coming to California. It seemed all hell had broken loose in the California Public School System. My first substitute-teaching job was in Burbank. I was unaware that the district was in the midst of a strike, and I would be crossing the picket line until I arrived at John Muir Junior High. There was no way I was going to cross a picket line, knowing that teachers are overworked and underpaid in the teaching profession. Therefore, I decided to apply as a substitute with Los Angeles Unified School District.

On my first assignment, I was sent to Locke High School. On my arrival, I saw yellow tape all around the corner of the school. I said to myself, *Oh, great they are filming a movie. Now, I will have something to write back to my sister and brother still living in Gary.* As I approached the office, I noticed for some strange reason all the classroom doors were closed. In Gary, we always kept our classroom doors open.

Finally, I arrived at the school's office and handed the secretary the substitute assignment sheet of paper. I asked, "By the way, what movie are they filming outside?" She looked at me, as if I were crazy! However, seeing the seriousness of my expression, she answered, "They're not filming a movie. That's a crime scene. Someone hung a woman in a tree last night." I almost fainted on the spot; I had to sit down quickly in the nearest chair. When I regrouped, I asked, "Why are the classroom doors closed?" She replied, "Lady, where are you from? The gangs are bad over here; you better lock your classroom door." I said, "Please, excuse me, but I cannot work at this school. Thank you very much." I never went back to L.A. Unified School District. I am not saying L.A. Unified School District was unsafe during that particular time, but gang activity was out of control, unlike Gary, where gangs were not like those in Los Angeles. It was a culture shock coming from one part of the country to another where things are totally different.

When my husband came home and I told him about that particular incident, he acted as if that was normal. I asked, "Are all the schools out here that bad?" He said he would check with his sister, and she would assist me in finding a position. In the meantime, my mother checked around and informed me that I had a first cousin working in the Compton School District, so I applied there. I was assigned to a middle school, which is the group of students I enjoy the most. I filled in for a teacher who was on maternity leave for the remainder of the school year. I was very excited. My mother babysat the twins, and Tyese and Turron were in Christian School all day.

You would not believe the first day on my teaching assignment. During my second period around 9:30 am, four police officers opened my classroom door and demanded that all my boys line up outside the door. They were told to spread eagle, to be searched for guns, knives, and brass knuckles. I thought I was in the "Wild, Wild West." I had never experienced anything like that in all my ten years of teaching. I was thinking surely these sweet little boys would not bring those things to school. Boy, was I in for a rude awakening. They found two handguns and three knives, but no brass knuckles. The students in possession of those items were handcuffed and taken to jail.

By the time my planning period began, students had told me so many horror stories (such as students' behavior in classrooms, where they think they are least likely to be punished). I could hardly walk without shaking. Every time I heard a loud noise, I immediately thought someone was shooting. I was a nervous wreck! In Gary, students were still respectful to anyone in authority. There were no gangs or "drive-by" shootings and surely not in the schools where I was from. Stories like these occurred on the South Side of Chicago, but not in Gary.

After conferring with a few teachers, they all said the same thing, "Just do your job. You cannot save the world. Tell the students not to bring any weapons to your class." As they were talking, I was saying to myself, *Tell them? You must be kidding!* I did not want to save the world. I wanted to teach students and give them the opportunity to become successful. You cannot do that in an environment where students are afraid for their lives, or where their teacher is scared for hers.

The principal of the school was dynamite, cool, calm, and immaculately dressed. The school ran like clockwork. Teachers were expected to greet all students at each changing class period, help move the students to their next class, and help in the lunchroom. She was always visible, checking each classroom making sure everything was running smoothly.

Often, the school would have a 'code yellow.' At that signal, all classroom doors are locked. No one was allowed out of the classroom, until an all-clear bell was rung. A 'code yellow' meant there was a gun on campus, a student had a gun, or someone not authorized to be on campus had entered. When I told my husband about all the drama, he suggested I find a nice quiet school. Where in California is a nice quiet school? He was so tired of the drama at my present school. He said he worried about me, while he was away from home, and it was affecting his job. Because we were not strapped for money and I stayed upset concerning the violence in California school, around the early 1980's, I decided to teach in the Archdioceses of Los Angeles. I taught seventh grade. Guess who was in the seventh grade? My daughter Tyese. Teaching in a private school afforded me the opportunity to be with my children all day. I was allowed to teach Tyese's seventh grade class and what a challenge that turned out to be.

Tyese thought because I was her mom and her teacher, I would give her some slack. Therefore, she would not complete or do her homework. One day, Tyese had not completed her homework, so as a punishment, I took away her recess time. Boy was she angry. After lunch, the students had to write an essay on the person they most admired and report to the class the next day. She must have thought of her plan all night.

The next day, the students took turns reporting to the rest of the class concerning the person they most admired. When Tyese's turned came, she said the person she most admired was Orville Redenbacher, the popcorn man, because of the delicious popcorn. I could have gone through the floor. However, Tyese did not know I was much smarter. Therefore, on the way home, I said, "Tyese, where would you like me to drop you off this evening? Do you know Orville's address?" She said, "No, I want to go home with you." I said, "I don't think so. I'm sure Orville would like to meet the person who admires him the most." When I saw the tears in her eyes, I knew I had made my point. We laugh about that to this day.

Tyese was not the only character in the family. Turron was a character as well. He was always in trouble in school. He was suspended in kindergarten for looking under the little girls' dresses. ***You reap what you sow!*** He had a temper just like his mother. I would spank him and punish him. I would take away his toys, but nothing worked. All through school, he fought. I enrolled him in football at an early age hoping that would give him something positive to do. The coaches encouraged him even more so to be even more aggressive. I even made him play basketball; it did not help his temper.

Turron went to Centennial High School, in the midst of gang violence, (late eighties and early nineties) and wore blue in a school where the students predominately wore red (students usually wore colors that matched the gangs in the surrounding area). Centennial High School colors are red, so to wear blue was frowned upon and may have led to serious consequences, which normally would get a student beat up or even shot. Turron did not care. His friends told me, "Nobody bothers Turron." They probably thought he was crazy!

After his graduation, I was told he had a baby on the way. As disappointed as I was, I thought the manly thing for him to do was to step up and be responsible. Well, right after high school, Turron enlisted into the United States Navy. That was the best move he ever made, because it quieted him down. I believe from those experiences he is now a very successful young man. I must add- through the prayers of his ancestors and mother, he is what he is today. Prayer had the greatest impact on his life.

Throughout my children's entire years of school, I was able to teach at the schools in which they were enrolled. When they reached the sixth grade, I felt I had nurtured them enough so they would be successful, if I was no longer at a school with them.

As I nurtured my children, Tyese developed her writing skills. Writing has always been one of her strengths. She graduated from Westchester High School in Los Angeles. She majored in Marketing. As a matter of fact, I am writing this book to motivate her to write her own. Melva and Melvin Jr. graduated from Mayfair High School in Lakewood, California. Melva graduated with a bachelor's degree in Psychology from Cal State Fullerton and has completed graduate school, majoring in psychology and obtaining her master's degree. In addition, Melvin Jr. is another story or another book. Keep him in your prayers. Melvin Eugene is going to preach the Gospel; therefore, he is running from God. However, we know all things work together for the good for those who love God.

I believe God has a perfect plan for every aspect of our lives. There is a time and season for reaping and sowing. There is a time to harvest. I believe as I grew mentally, I also grew spiritually. A good Word preaching church was all I needed. I have learned to stop blaming my biological father for my situations and attitudes. I have learned that my real father will always be Father God, and He is the only Father I will ever need. Once I learned God has a purpose for my life, nothing will ever keep me from fulfilling that purpose. I want to share with you my readers, these facts because I have come a long way from where I started.

I take all issues of abuse seriously because I was abused myself mentally. I was abused by the reactions of adults in my family, the media, schools, and even in the church. I lived by social standards I could never reach. I believed the lies of the devil. At least that is what I thought, and then one day as if I was struck my lightening, I made up my mind that nothing would be impossible, as long as I trusted in my Heavenly Father and believe He is God Almighty.

As you read the life I presented, my overall point was God has a purpose for each and everyone. We need to move over and let God take the driver's seat. We need to learn to stop giving Him the directions we want for our lives and know He had our destiny already planned before we were in our mother's womb.

Ephesians 2:10 says, *"For we are his workmanship, created in Christ Jesus unto good works, which God hath before ordained that we should walk in them."*

I want to take you back to the image of me sitting on those steps waiting for "Black" to show up. Even in my little mind, God had planted greatness. He is not through with me yet, for I still have a way to go. I have placed in this novel everything that came across my life, all the pieces of my puzzle that have led me to the place I am today.

My life was a puzzle because I had no idea who I was and where I was going.

I am a strong believer that one must find him/herself in order to understand the path that God is directing him/her onto. I have shared my story beginning with me not knowing who I was, including where I came from and knowing nothing about my ancestors. If you do not know who you are, you definitely cannot figure out where you are going. Not only did I not have God in my life, I did not know who I was, nor the plans God had for my life. It took years to finally get over my mistakes and turn them into stepping stones that have made me the woman I am today.

When I was a child, one of the most influential persons in my life was my great-grandmother (as I shared earlier). She assisted me on my spiritual journey by teaching me what she knew. For example, Nana had a book with illustrations of African people with large bones through their noses, lips, and ears. They had scars cut into their faces. She showed me pictures of the Pigmy Tribes, who were shorter than five feet and Zulu tribes who were six feet or taller. I was scared of that book and often had nightmares about the people I saw in that book. Nana had only gone as far as third grade in school because she had to pick cotton to help support her family. However, her husband had taught her to read and compute. Nana could count money very rapidly, adding, subtracting, and multiplying.

Once when we were at a store, Nana bought bologna and crackers. The bill should have been a dollar. Nana handed the man a five-dollar bill, and he gave her two dollars in change. When she questioned the man about her change, he tried to run a con game. He did not know who Nana was or who he was dealing with. She must have grabbed that man's arm so hard that he hurried up and gave her the correct change. Then, he had the nerve to tell Nana not to come back to his store. I am so glad I was with Nana, because Nana gave that man a look, and I know Nana was either going to meet her maker or go to jail. I quickly said, "Come, Nana. We don't like this store anyway!"

Looking back over my life, I clearly understand the lessons I learned on this spiritual journey. It was always His plan to develop me in His image. I also realized the areas in which I failed some tests and had to take the tests over. As I observed the historical events I experienced in my past, they also developed me into a better person. I am always pointing out the injustices I still observe, the violence, the racism, and blatant discrimination still visible today. I also want to leave a legacy for my children, grandchildren and great-grandchildren, so they will always be reminded of their ancestry.

Most importantly, I want those of you who have been through similar situations in your lives or are going through at the present to know that you do not have to go through it alone. God is waiting for you to call on Him, and He will direct your paths. He is *not* a man that He should lie. What He says in His word, He is more than able to provide.

Dr. Stacey Nickleberry

Chapter 26
Closing Thoughts

I thank God for making a way for me. I truly thank my mother for being a remarkable woman and laying a solid foundation as I watched her provide for her family without complaint, as she made sure her children had the best her money could buy. All these things made me realize that she is the kind of woman I wanted to be. I may not have done everything right, lacking a real biological father, BUT, when I finally realized the only father I always needed was always there in my heart (and it took Him sometime to break through all the coldness, blockages, closures, and mess I wrapped around my heart to make sure no one would ever get to it again), I asked for forgiveness for hurting people by not letting them near my heart because of my negative attitude. "I'll do you before you do me!" was my attitude. I am so glad I am over and done with that. Thank you, heavenly Father for being the ONLY father I ever needed to lead me to such a wonderful life, full of people who love me unconditionally. Again, I thank you!

Presently, I am finishing my course work and writing my dissertation for a Ph.D. in Higher Education Administration. The picture below represents that celebration.

To God be the glory for all He has done!

Dr. Stacey Nickleberry

About the Author

Dr. Stacey Nickleberry has over thirty-years of experience as an educator and administrator. She was a classroom teacher for grades K-12 before serving as an administrator. She retired from the public school system as a middle school principal. In preparation for her career, she attended Indiana University, where she earned a Bachelor's Degree in Sociology and United States History and a Master's Degree in Secondary Education. Further, she earned an Administrative Credential from La Verne University, in La Verne, California. Dr. Nickleberry also taught and supervised aspiring teachers in the master's program, as well as undergraduate history courses, at the University of Phoenix. She is presently completing a Ph.D. in Higher Education Administration at the University of Phoenix.

Dr. Stacey Nickleberry is the mother of four children: Tyese, Turron, Melva, and Melvin, Jr. She is the stepmother of LaVon Nickleberry and Jacque Nickleberry Hughes. She has five grand-children and two great-grandchildren.

Because of the Heavenly Father, Dr. Stacey Nickleberry is experiencing, peace, love, joy, and happiness regardless of her past trials and tribulations. She is an overcomer!

Join Dr. Stacey on *Facebook* to discuss the issues that were raised in her book at:
www.facebook.com/NobodysDaughterByDr.StaceyNickleberry

Share your own personal experiences with other women and become a means of support. Dr. Stacey is looking forward to conversing with you today!

References

19th Century History About.com (http://history1800s.about.com/od/1800sglossary/g/Sharecropping-def.htm)

Civil Wrongs- The Klu Klux Klan blacksphere.net/2013/06/civil-wrongs-the-ku-klux-klan

James Brown Biography http://www.rollingstone.com/music/artists/jamesbrown/biography#ixzz2fDGeKyMO

London, Jack. Hobo History

Mardis Gras New Orleans. www.mardigrasneworleans.com/history.html

Pullman History.http://www.pullman-museum.org/sleepingcars at sbcglobal.net

Signs and Symptoms of Anger swayamsat.org/blog.item.20/signs-symptoms-of-anger.html

www.ingramcontent.com/pod-product-compliance
Lightning Source LLC
LaVergne TN
LVHW051645080426
835511LV00016B/2500